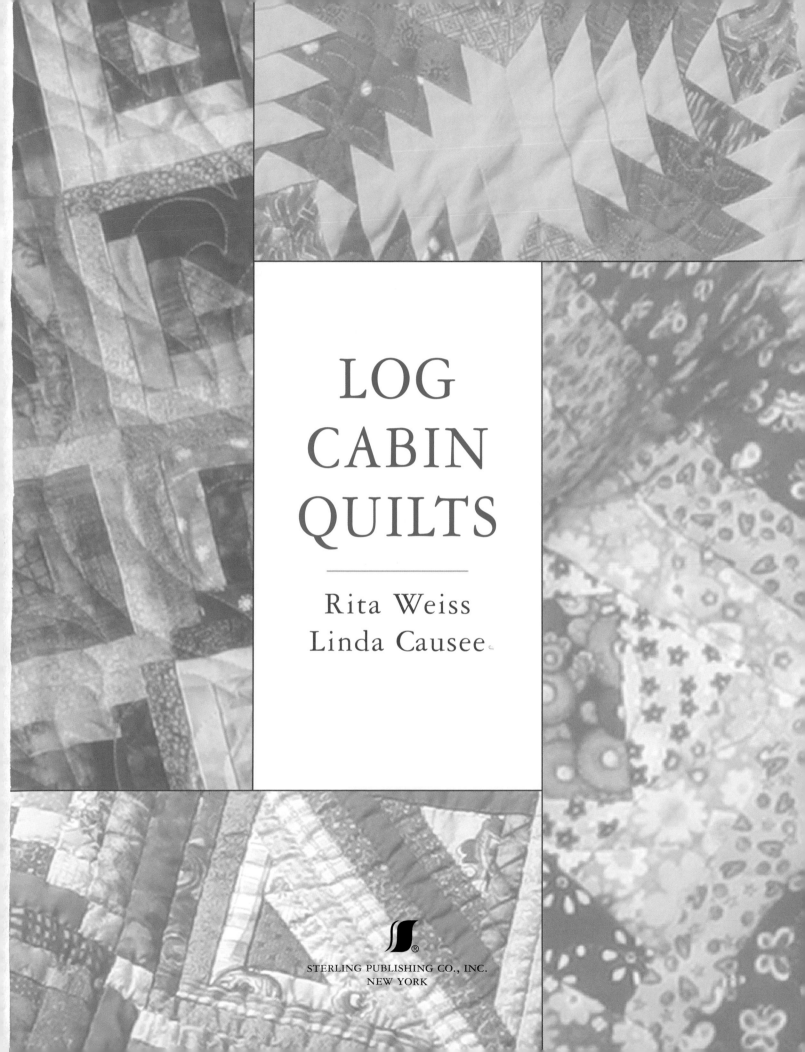

LOG CABIN QUILTS

Rita Weiss
Linda Causee

STERLING PUBLISHING CO., INC.
NEW YORK

Produced by: The Creative Partners,™ LLC
Book Design: Joyce Lerner
Photo Stylist: Carol Wilson Mansfield
Photography: Wayne Norton
Technical Editor: Ann Harnden

Many thanks to the following for their work in piecing the quilts:
Linda Ferguson, Harriet Fox, Dawn Kallunki, Ada Le Claire,
Wanda MacLachlan, April McArthur, and Mary K. Randall

Special thanks to:
Faith Horsky who quilted many of the quilts, to Sandy Boobar, who quilted *Logs and Nine Patches,*
and to Harriet Fox, who quilted *Gone Fishin'.*

*The following companies generously supplied their products
for the projects in this book:*

Fairfield Processing Corp.:
Cotton Classic Batting
Northcott Silks, Inc.:
Artisan's Palette by Ro Gregg for *Log Cabin Stars and Triangles*
Wild Iris by Ro Gregg for *Bordering on Log Cabins*
Sun, Moon and Stars by Janet Orfini for *Celestial Star Log Cabin*
Maywood Studio:
Woodsman in Spring by Perry Wahe for *Gone Fishin'*
Robert Kaufman:
Nature's Brilliance collection for *Logs and Nine Patches*

Library of Congress Cataloging-in-Publication Data Available

10 9 8 7 6 5 4 3 2 1

Published by Sterling Publishing Co., Inc.
387 Park Avenue South, New York, NY 10016
© 2006 by The Creative Partners™ LLC
Distributed in Canada by Sterling Publishing
c/o Canadian Manda Group, 165 Dufferin Street,
Toronto, Ontario, Canada M6K 3H6
Distributed in the United Kingdom by GMC Distribution Services,
Castle Place, 166 High Street, Lewes, East Sussex, England BN7 1XU
Distributed in Australia by Capricorn Link (Australia) Pty. Ltd.
P.O. Box 704, Windsor, NSW 2756, Australia

Printed in China
All rights reserved

Sterling ISBN-13: 978-1-4027-2312-4
ISBN-10: 1-4027-2312-1

For information about custom editions, special sales, premium and
corporate purchases, please contact Sterling Special Sales
Department at 800-805-5489 or specialsales@sterlingpub.com.

We Love Log Cabins!

Whenever we're called upon to make a quilt—whether it's a present for a newborn or a retirement gift—Log Cabins always come first to mind. Not only are they quick to make, but there are so many different variations that new patterns constantly appear.

The World's Easiest Log Cabin

Linda likes to make her Log Cabins by using the foundation piecing method while Rita, being the old-fashioned one of the duo, prefers the traditional strip-piecing method. Although in this collection, Rita did succumb to the ease of foundation piecing when the self-imposed deadline loomed. Linda, on the other hand, decided that her *Alaska Rag* quilt, made of flannel, would work better if she strip pieced it.

Our love for Log Cabins assured us that many of our quilting friends had as warm a place in their quilting hearts as we did for this wonderful pattern. Just a simple request, and what wonderful quilts turned up. Stacy Michell delighted us with *The World's Easiest Log Cabin* while Sharon Hultgren's *Log Cabin Cubes* showed us that a Log Cabin doesn't have to be "square," and Nancy Brenan Daniel's *Ladybug, Ladybug* really made us grin. Margrette Carr amazed us with the very first Log Cabin she had ever made, *Antique Log Cabin Revisited,* proving once again that even a beginner can make a magnificent Log Cabin.

Log Cabin Cubes

Marti Michell shared with us her *Gone Fishin'*, a quilt made with a new ruler she had just developed to make Log Cabins even easier to create. Dori Hawks, who had spent the past winter in what she called a "log cabin marathon," producing Log Cabins, was delighted to send us her *Purple Pineapple.* Ann Harnden's innovative *Split Logs* and Christina Jensen's *Logs and Nine Patches* showed us that there is no end to the creativity inspired by that simple Log Cabin pattern.

We owe a thanks to all of our quilting friends and especially to Flavin Glover, the grande dame of Log Cabin, without whom a book on Log Cabin quilts would not be complete. Flavin's *Spring Star* is actually seven different Log Cabin blocks combined into one masterpiece.

Spring Star

The Log Cabin quilt in all its many forms is completely fascinating. Today many quilt artists are able to take the basic form that has been here for over 100 years and use it as a jumping-off point for some very creative designs. In some cases the original Log Cabin block is completely discernable; in others it may be difficult to see the original concept, but the block is still there constantly inspiring new quit artists.

Rita Weiss   Linda Causee

14

36

108

22

18

CONT

E N T S

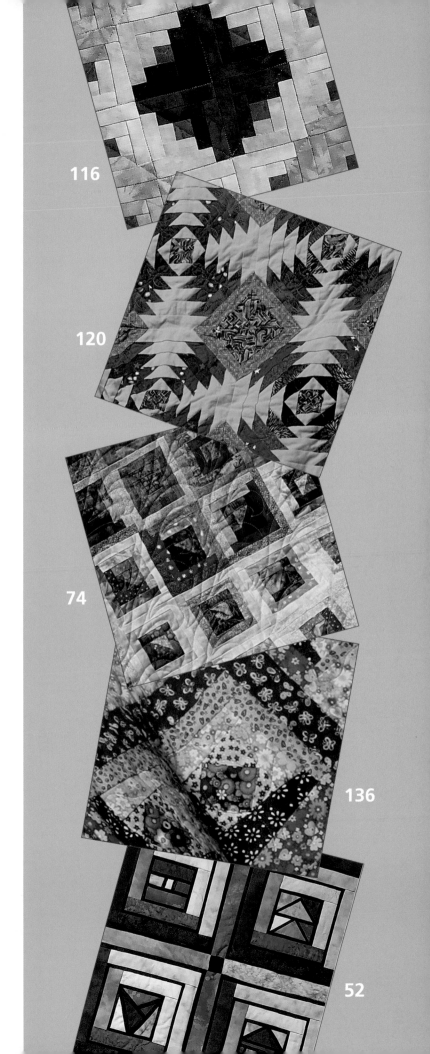

116

120

74

136

52

Quilt names—especially those applied to this most popular of quilts—reflected the day-to-day life of the pioneers. A barn raising was a joyous community occasion. **Diagram 4** honors this tradition with the "Barn Raising" quilt. The same traditional blocks shown in **Diagram 1** are created but set in such a manner as to create a dark center surrounded by a light and dark borders in the same orderly fashion that was used to complete the barn.

Straight Furrows

Diagram 5

Barn Raising

Diagram 4

The pioneers on the prairie worked their farms, and the "Straight Furrows" in **Diagram 5** were reminiscent of the plowed fields.

Turn the "Straight Furrows" blocks into a different pattern, and the quilt becomes "Pinwheels" as in **Diagram 6**.

Diagram 6

Pinwheels

Making the "Pinwheel" blocks of only two colors as in **Diagram 7** creates an entirely different version.

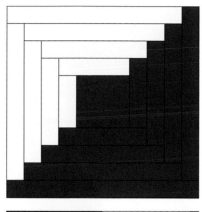

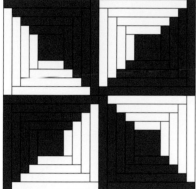

Diagram 7

If the two-color blocks used in the quilt are the same color (**Diagram 8**), the quilt takes on a different look than if half the blocks are made of a two-color version leaving the other half to be made of another color choice as in **Diagram 9**.

Diagram 8

Diagram 9

9

By rearranging the strips, the quilter gives birth to other interesting and colorful versions of the Log Cabin block. Here instead of placing all the light fabrics around one side of the center and all of the dark fabrics around the other side, "Courthouse Steps" (**Diagram 10**) puts the dark fabrics on one side and the light fabrics on the other two sides, creating the steps that lead up to the town courthouse.

Diagram 11 shows a number of different versions that can be created with "Courthouse Steps".

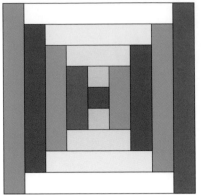

Diagram 10

Courthouse Steps

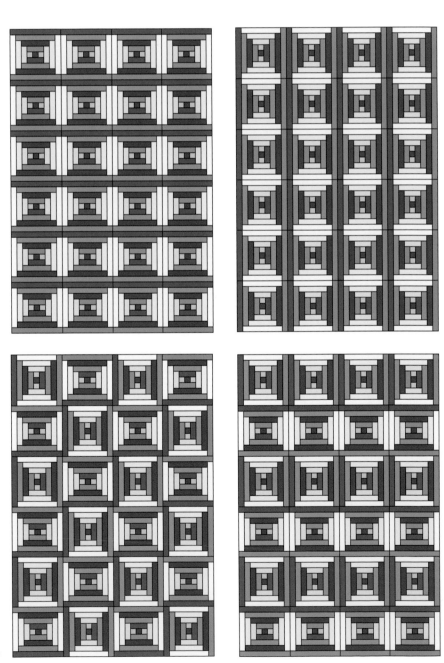

Diagram 11

In a variation of "Courthouse Steps" we find another block, "Chimneys and Cornerstones" (**Diagram 12**). In this block, a contrasting square is placed in the corners where light and dark fabrics meet. When these blocks are combined as in **Diagram 13**, a diagonal grid is created.

Diagram 12

Chimneys & Cornerstones

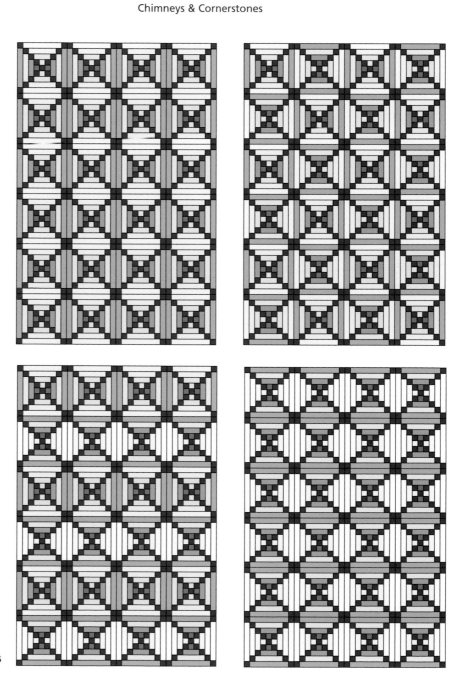

Diagram 13

11

By placing the center square in the top corner of the block and then adding the strips along two sides of the center square, another variation of the Log Cabin block, the "Chevron" is created (**Diagram 14**). Placed adjacent to each other, the chevron pattern is revealed as in **Diagram 15**. This version of the "Log Cabin", however, can be combined in many different ways to create other amazing combinations as seen in **Diagram 16**.

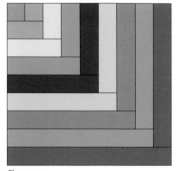

Chevron

Diagram 14

Diagram 15

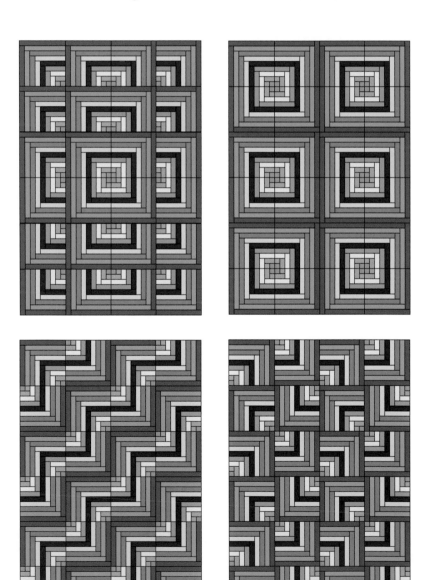

Diagram 16

Never satisfied with endlessly making patterns with little variations, really creative quilt makers turned the Log Cabin block around and created a first cousin of the Log Cabin called the "Pineapple" (**Diagram 17**). By moving the block around in many creative ways, the quilter ended up with quilts that had movement as in **Diagram 18**.

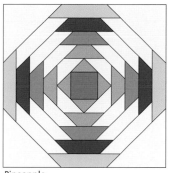

Diagram 17

Pineapple

Diagram 18

13

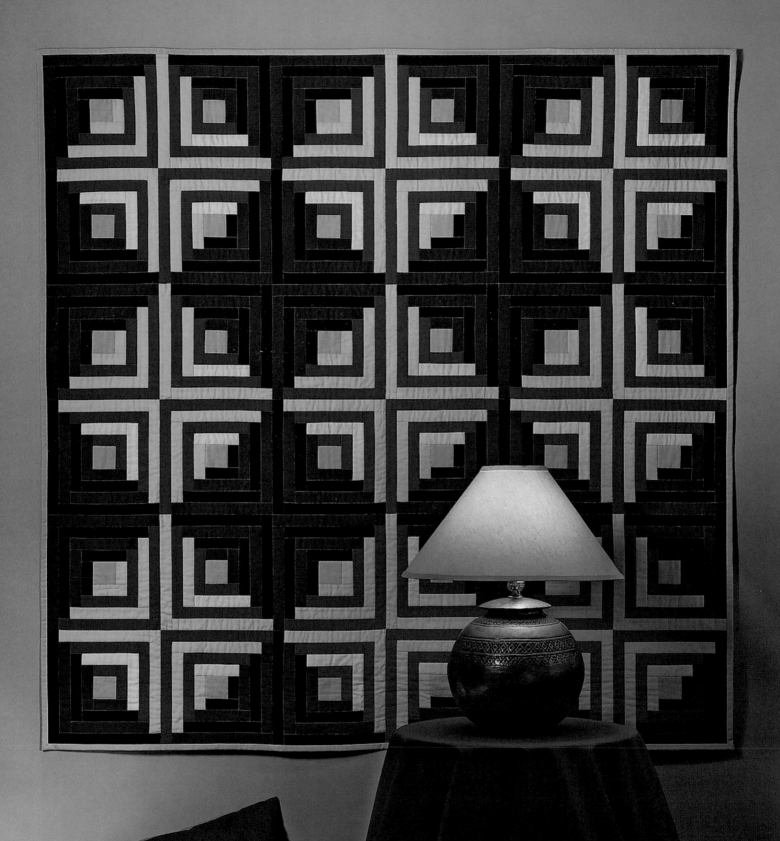

An antique quilt made in Pennsylvania in 1885 was the inspiration for this traditional Log Cabin quilt. If the original pink does not appeal to you, try making this quilt in other colors of your choice.

Antique Log Cabin Revisited

by Margrette Carr

Approximate Size
61" x 61"

Size of Block
10" finished

Materials
$1^1/8$ yds each red, yellow, navy, burgundy (logs)
$7/8$ yd pink (centers, binding)
3 yds backing
batting

Cutting
Blocks
36 squares, $2^1/2$" x $2^1/2$", pink (centers)
from each of the red, yellow, navy and burgundy, cut:
    9 strips, $1^1/2$" x $2^1/2$" (log 1)
    18 strips, $1^1/2$" x $3^1/2$" (logs 2, 3)
    18 strips, $1^1/2$" x $4^1/2$" (logs 4, 5)
    18 strips, $1^1/2$" x $5^1/2$" (logs 6, 7)
    18 strips, $1^1/2$" x $6^1/2$" (logs 8, 9)
    18 strips, $1^1/2$" x $7^1/2$" (logs 10, 11)
    18 strips, $1^1/2$" x $8^1/2$" (logs 12, 13)
    18 strips, $1^1/2$" x $9^1/2$" (logs 14, 15)
    9 strips, $1^1/2$" x $10^1/2$" (log 16)

Finishing
6 strips, 3"-wide, pink (binding)

Margrette Carr has been quilting for over ten years. Her work has won a number of awards and has been displayed in quilt shows across the country. Five of her quilts were used in a book written by Pat Yamin entitled *Back to Basics*. In addition two of her quilts were featured on a popular TV quilt show.

This is actually the first Log Cabin quilt Margrette has ever made. She enjoyed working on it so much that she plans to add many more to her collection!

Instructions

Note: *Refer to Making a Log Cabin Block, pages 146 to 147, before beginning.*

1. Lay out nine each of four different blocks, alternating red/yellow on two sides and navy/burgundy on the other two sides. (**Diagram 1**)

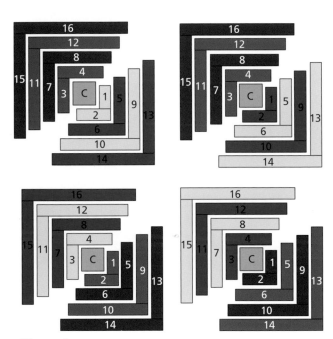

Diagram 1

2. Using accurate $^1/4$" seams and starting in the center with the pink square and shortest log, piece all the blocks, pressing seams away from the center. (**Diagram 2**)

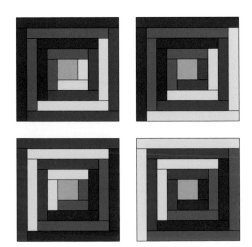

Diagram 2

3. Make four stacks of nine identical blocks with the red/yellow sides toward the center. (**Diagram 3**)

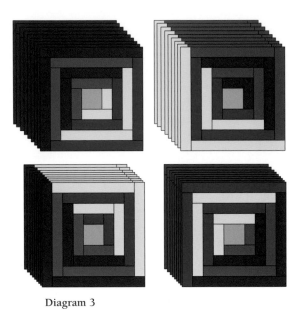

Diagram 3

4. Sew blocks together in pairs then sew pairs together. (**Diagram 4**)

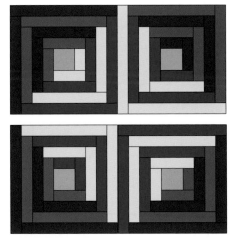

Diagram 4

Diagram 5

5. Sew blocks together to finish the top. (**Diagram 5**)

6. Refer to Finishing Your Quilt, pages 154 to 159, to complete your quilt. **Note:** *The photographed quilt was machine quilted with heavy pink variegated thread in the ditch of every seam. Strips for binding are 3"-wide.*

Antique Log Cabin
Revisited Quilt Layout

Triangle-shaped blocks make the star in this quilt. The placement of the medium blue, aqua and purple prints in the blocks creates circles within the star. While the quilt looks complex, it is actually very simple to construct using the foundation-piecing method.

Log Cabin Stars and Triangles

by Linda Causee

Approximate Size
53$^{1}/_{2}$" x 60"

Materials
$^{5}/_{8}$ yard fuchsia (includes first border)
$^{5}/_{8}$ yard medium aqua
$^{5}/_{8}$ yard light yellow
$^{1}/_{4}$ yard medium blue
$^{1}/_{2}$ yard purple
1 yard dark blue (includes second border)
1$^{1}/_{8}$ yards light blue
1$^{1}/_{8}$ yards light aqua
$^{1}/_{2}$ yard binding
3$^{1}/_{8}$ yards backing
batting

Patterns
Log Cabin Foundation/Triangle, page 20

Cutting
Blocks
Note: *You do not have to cut exact pieces when foundation piecing. Cut strips in the widths shown below for easier piecing.*

3 strips, 1$^{7}/_{8}$"-wide, fuchsia
17 strips, 1"-wide, medium aqua
19 strips, 1"-wide, light yellow
6 strips, 1"-wide, medium blue
11 strips, 1"-wide, purple
6 strips, 1"-wide, dark blue

Finishing
28 Triangles, light blue
28 Triangles, light aqua

Although **Linda Causee** had been editing quilt books since 1990, it wasn't until 1992 after attending a workshop with Marti Michell using her quilt-as-you-go technique that she made her first Log Cabin quilt. That started Linda creating Log Cabin books as fast as she could dream up new patterns. Some of her titles include: *101 Log Cabin Blocks, 202 Little Log Cabin Blocks,* and *101 Log Cabin Flowers.*

Married for 25 years to Rick Causee, Linda has two grown children, Christopher who is a Lieutenant Junior Grade in the US Navy and Kathryn who is in her second year of college. Angel, their adorable pug puppy who helped Linda through the empty nest syndrome, rounds out the family.

6 strips, 2"-wide, fuchsia (first border)
6 strips, 4"-wide, dark blue (second border)
6 strips, 2¹/2"-wide, binding

Instructions

1. Make 48 Triangle Log Cabin foundations refer-ring to Preparing the Foundation, page 151. (**Diagram 1**)

2. Referring to Making a Foundation Block, pages 152 to 154, piece the block in the amounts shown for the color arrangements in **Diagram 2**.

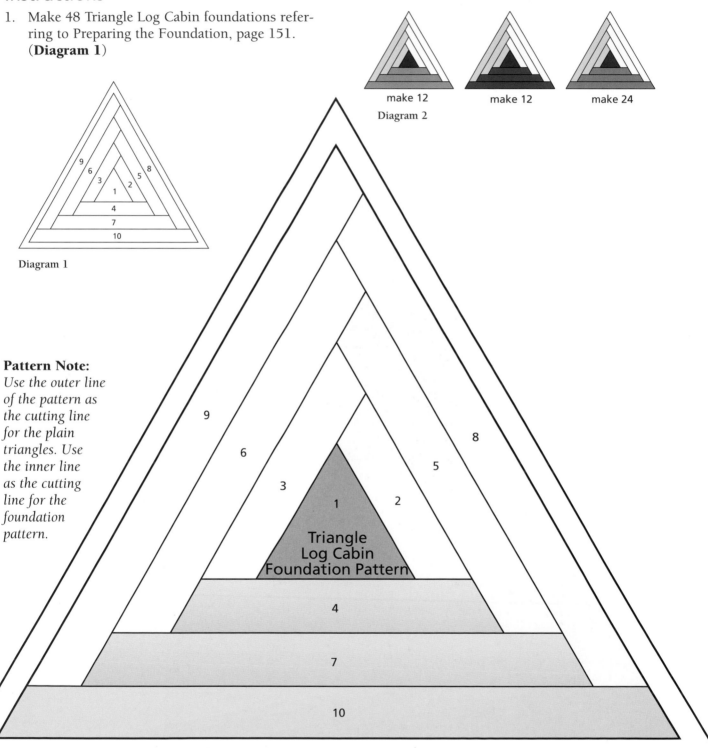

make 12   make 12   make 24

Diagram 2

Diagram 1

Pattern Note:
Use the outer line of the pattern as the cutting line for the plain triangles. Use the inner line as the cutting line for the foundation pattern.

9
6
3
1   2
5
8
Triangle
Log Cabin
Foundation Pattern
4
7
10

Log Cabin Triangle Foundation Pattern/Triangle Pattern

Diagram 3

3. Place blocks and triangles referring to **Diagram 3**. Sew into rows then sew rows together. Trim sides of quilt top $1/4$" from inner points of triangles.

4. Measure quilt top lengthwise; cut 2"-wide fuchsia strips to that length. Sew to sides of quilt. Measure quilt top crosswise; cut 2"-wide fuchsia strips to that length. Sew to top and bottom of quilt.

5. Repeat step 4 for second border using 4"-wide dark blue strips.

6. Refer to Finishing Your Quilt, page 154 to 159, to complete your quilt.

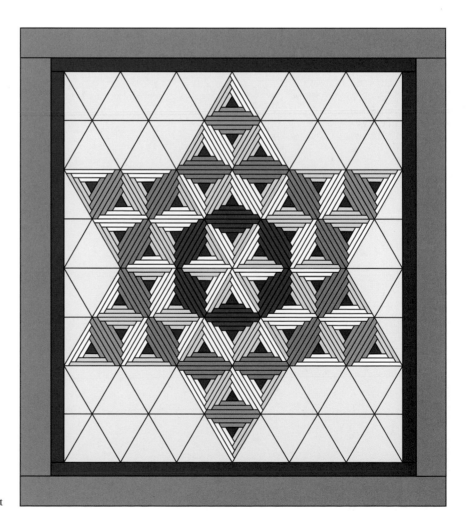

Log Cabin Stars and
Triangles Quilt Layout

The basic construction of the blocks in this quilt relies on a modified Log Cabin technique. The strips are stitched around the block in a spiral direction, and it doesn't matter which direction as long as the direction is consistent. To create the details within the blocks, the basic Log Cabin technique is stopped now and then to sew and flip a corner triangle onto the block to create a leaf or a lady bug. It's fun and fast. Reserve all of the scraps until the quilt is finished.

Ladybug, Ladybug

by Nancy Brenan Daniel

Approximate Size
42" x 52"

Materials
1³/4 yards background print
¹/2 yard light green
¹/2 yard medium green
¹/4 yard assorted scraps of violet
fat quarter medium red
fat quarter bright red
scraps pink
scrap black
¹/8 yard orange
1¹/4 yards dark floral print (border and binding)
2 yards backing
batting

Templates
A, B, C and D, pages 28, 29

Cutting
Note: *Cut five 2¹/4"-wide strips each of the two green fabrics. From these strips cut leaf rectangles and use the remaining sections for the pieced border.*

Block #1 – Leaf
3 squares, 5³/4" x 5³/4", background print (center)
9 squares, 2¹/4" x 2¹/4", background print
3 rectangles, 2¹/4" x 5³/4", light green (log 1)
3 rectangles, 2¹/4" x 7¹/2", medium green (log 2)

Block #2 – Flowers
1 strip, 1¹/2" x 18", orange (centers)
1 strip, 1¹/4"-wide, background print (log 1)

Trained as an art educator and art historian, **Nancy Brenan Daniel** has had a lifelong interest in the practice of quilting as an art form. She absorbed her love of quilts and her early quilting skills from her maternal grandmother who encouraged her to play with fabric and templates and to sew at a very young age.

In 1975 she began teaching quilt making through her local Parks Department in anticipation of the United States Bicentennial, and in 1982, she opened the Quilters' Ranch in Tempe, Arizona. Along with her two business partners, she expanded the successful business twice in ten years before she sold her portion to her partners. Now she devotes herself to quilt making, teaching, judging, designing and writing more than 20 books and articles on sewing and quilt making. Her quilts have appeared on the covers of several calendars and have been featured in many magazines and books.

As a National Quilters' Association certified quilt judge, she is frequently called upon to judge competitions and to deliver lectures and workshops.

The mother of three grown children and grandmother of three, she still finds time from her busy schedule to volunteer in her community and to be the faithful companion to her two "furkids": Toby, the Airedale, and Sashie, the Border Collie-mix.

Block #3 – Ladybugs

Note: *There are five Ladybug Blocks. Only two are exactly alike! Pay attention.*

1. Chain piece the bright and medium red triangles together. (**Diagram 13**) Cut apart and press seam open.

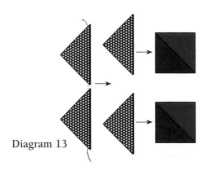

Diagram 13

2. Stitch and flip a Template B black square onto the corner of each red Ladybug square. (**Diagram 14**)

Diagram 14

3. Stitch and flip three Template C background squares to the remaining corners of the red square. (**Diagram 15**)

Diagram 15

4. Create the black Ladybug spots with either a permanent fabric marker, paint, or use a stencil with black fabric paint to make spots. (**Diagram 16**)

Diagram 16

5. Add logs 1, 2, 3 and 4 in same manner as for the Flower blocks. Stitch and flip 2$^{1}/4$" background print squares to complete Ladybug blocks. (**Diagram 17**)

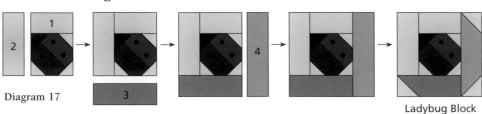

Diagram 17

Ladybug Block
Make 2

Note: *Pay close attention to the change in placement of the green fabrics and Bugs.* (**Diagram 18**)

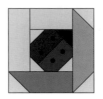 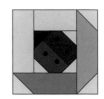

Ladybug Block B
Make 1

Ladybug Block C
Make 1

Ladybug Block D
Make 1

Diagram 18

Block #4 – House

1. Stitch and flip two Template C background squares onto opposite corners of the 4" red square. (**Diagram 19**)

Diagram 19

2. Paint, stencil or use a permanent marker for the door to the house. (**Diagram 20**)

Diagram 20

3. Sew orange rectangles (logs 1 and 2) to adjacent sides of red square for the roof. (**Diagram 21**)

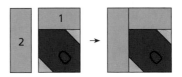

Diagram 21

26

4. Sew a 2$1/4$" x 5$3/4$" medium green rectangle (log 3) and 2$1/4$" x 7$1/2$" light green rectangle (log 4) to complete Log Cabin round. Using stitch and flip, sew 2$1/4$" background print squares to light and medium green rectangles to complete block. (**Diagram 22**)

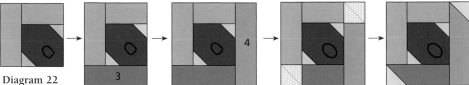

Diagram 22

Finishing

1. Lay out the blocks in diagonal rows referring to **Diagram 23**. Fill in with setting and corner triangles.

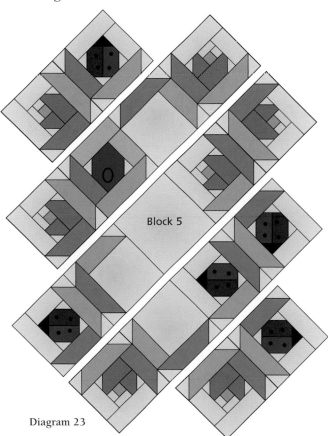

Block 5

Diagram 23

2. Sew blocks together in rows then sew rows together. Press seams opposite each other in each row. (**Diagram 24**)

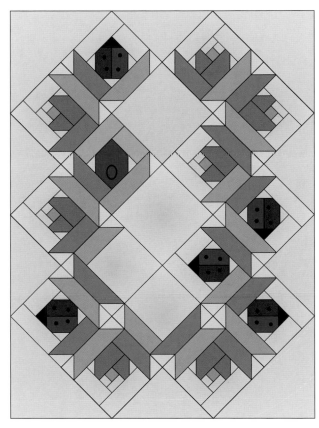

Diagram 24

3. **Optional:** *Using embroidery, paint, permanent marker or stencils create Ladybug antenna and flower pollen.* (**Diagram 25**)

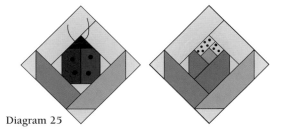

Diagram 25

4. Trim the quilt top to create straight, regular edges and corners.

5. *Pieced Border:* Sew the Template D triangles to the Template C orange squares. Press. (**Diagram 26**)

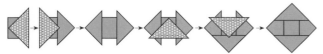

Diagram 26

6. Trim to 2^1/4" x 2^1/4" squares. (**Diagram 27**)

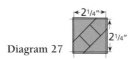

Diagram 27

7. **Optional:** *Complete center of the flowers with a machine or hand blanket stitch.* (**Diagram 28**)

Diagram 28

8. Sew 2^1/4"-wide light and medium green strips diagonally. Use random lengths of strips. (**Diagram 29**)

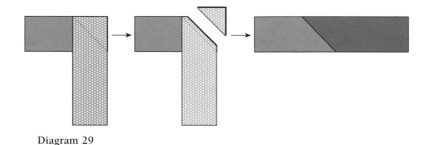

Diagram 29

9. Sew pieced strips to flowers to create the pieced border. The placement of the flowers should be random. See the photo and layout for a better illustration.

10. Measure the quilt top lengthwise. Cut two pieced border strips to that length. Sew to sides of quilt.

11. Measure the quilt crosswise. Cut two pieced border strips to that length. Sew to top and bottom of quilt.

12. Measure quilt top as in steps 10 and 11 and attach 5"-wide dark floral strips for second border.

13. Refer to Finishing Your Quilt, pages 154 to 159, to complete your quilt.

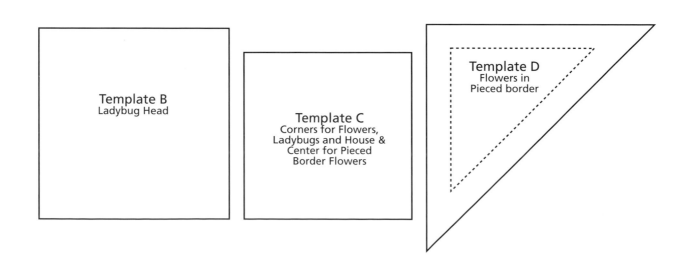

Template B
Ladybug Head

Template C
Corners for Flowers,
Ladybugs and House &
Center for Pieced
Border Flowers

Template D
Flowers in
Pieced border

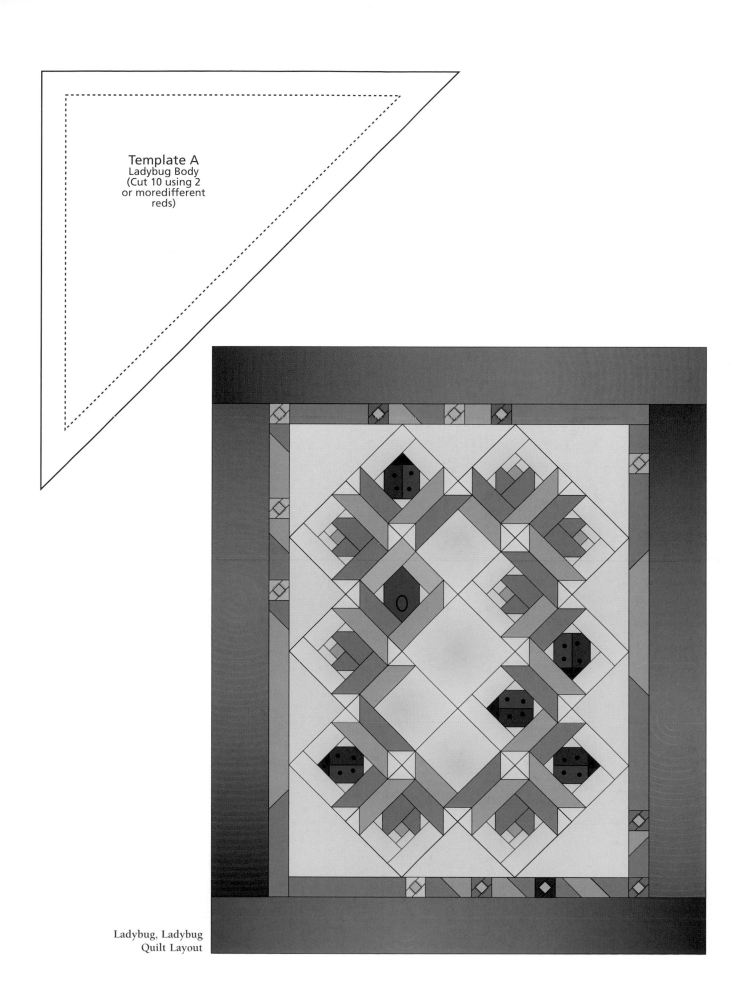

Template A
Ladybug Body
(Cut 10 using 2
or moredifferent
reds)

Ladybug, Ladybug
Quilt Layout

In this quilt the Log Cabin block is used creatively to make a border. By utilizing a diamond-shape block, the designer has actually created a border that looks like a braided chain. The traditional Log Cabin blocks in the center of the quilt, made from the Wild Iris collection of fabric by Northcott Silks, create a subtle garden.

Bordering on Log Cabins

by Linda Causee

Approximate Size
$36^1/2$" x $36^1/2$"

Materials
$1/2$ yard green floral (includes second border)
$3/8$ yard beige floral
$1/4$ yard light purple
$1/4$ yard light blue
$5/8$ yard beige
$1/4$ yard light pink
$1/4$ yard light green
$3/8$ yard dark blue
$3/8$ yard dark purple
$1/4$ yard dark green (first border)
$1/4$ yard dark pink (third border)
$3/8$ yard binding
$1^1/8$ yards backing
batting

Patterns
Log Cabin Block, page 34
Log Cabin Border, page 34
Corner Block, page 35

Cutting
Log Cabin Blocks
16 squares, 2" x 2", green floral (center 1)
2 strips, $1^1/4$"-wide, beige floral (logs 2, 3)
2 strips, $1^1/4$"-wide, light purple (log 4)

Linda Causee never planned to become a quilter even though she enjoyed doing crafts, especially embroidery and sewing. After receiving a BA in Biology from the University of California in San Diego, Linda planned to work for a year and then go on to graduate school. Instead she met her husband, married and had her first child. She never went back to school.

While her children were young, Linda sewed their clothes and made a few simple patchwork baby quilts. In addition she worked at a local fabric store and fell in love with fabric.

A local needlework publishing company hired her to make models and eventually asked her to take a full-time job. Within a year, she was promoted to quilt editor, and she found the work she loved the most.

2 strips, 1¼"-wide, light blue (log 5)
4 strips, 1¼"-wide, beige (logs 6, 7)
2 strips, 1¼"-wide, light pink (log 8)
3 strips, 1¼"-wide, light green (log 9)
5 strips, 1¼"-wide, beige floral (logs 10, 11)
3 strips, 1¼"-wide, dark blue (log 12)
3 strips, 1¼"-wide, dark purple (log 13)

Log Cabin Border blocks
2 strips, 1⅞"-wide, green floral (center 1)
3 strips, ⅞"-wide, light pink (logs 2, 5)
3 strips, ⅞"-wide, light green (logs 3, 4)
4 strips, ⅞"-wide, light blue (logs 6, 9)
4 strips, ⅞"-wide, light purple (logs 7, 8)
5 strips, ⅞"-wide, dark purple (logs 10, 13)
5 strips, ⅞"-wide, dark blue (logs 11, 12)
8 strips, 1⅝"-wide, beige (spaces 14, 15, 16, 17)

Corner blocks
4 squares, 3½" x 3½", beige (space 1)
1 strip, ⅞"-wide, dark purple (space 2)
1 strip, ⅞"-wide, dark blue (space 3)
4 squares, 1½" x 1½", beige (space 4)

Finishing
4 strips, 1¼"-wide, dark green (first border)
4 strips, 1¾"-wide, green floral (second border)
4 strips, 1½"-wide, dark pink (third border)
4 strips, 2½"-wide, binding

Instructions

Note: *Read Foundation Piecing a Log Cabin Block, pages 151 to 154, before making blocks.*

1. Make 16 Log Cabin block, 20 Log Cabin Border blocks, and four Corner block foundations referring to Preparing the Foundation, page 151. (**Diagram 1**)

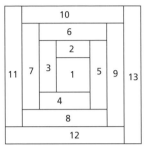

make 16

make 4

Diagram 1

make 20

2. Referring to Making the Foundation Block, page 152 to 154, piece all blocks referring to the pattern for placement of colors. (**Diagram 2**)

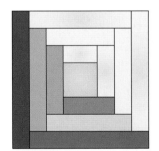

Diagram 2

3. Place Log Cabin blocks in four rows of four blocks. Sew together in row then sew rows together. (**Diagram 3**)

Diagram 3

4. Measure quilt lengthwise; it should measure $24^1/2$". Cut two $1^1/4$"-wide dark green strips to that length. Sew to sides of quilt. Measure quilt crosswise; it should measure 26". Cut two $1^1/4$"-wide dark green strips to that length. Sew to top and bottom of quilt.

5. Repeat step 4 for second border with $1^3/4$"-wide green floral strips and third border with $1^1/2$"-wide dark pink strips.

6. Sew five Log Cabin border blocks together; repeat three more times. (**Diagram 4**)

Diagram 4

7. Sew a Log Cabin border to opposite sides of quilt top. (**Diagram 5**)

Diagram 5

8. Sew Corner blocks to each end of remaining Log Cabin borders; sew to top and bottom of quilt. (**Diagram 6**)

Diagram 5

9. Refer to Finishing Your Quilt, pages 154 to 159 to complete your quilt.

This quilt is a sampler of Log Cabin blocks filled with an array of printed and solid fabrics. The yellow cornerstones form a strong diagonal pattern across the quilt. The cornerstones also divide the blue and green fabrics that project the same color value in the quilt. The quilt contains seven different Log Cabin blocks.

Spring Star
by Flavin Glover

Approximate Size
65" x 65"

Materials
9 fat quarters, assorted royal blue
9 fat quarters assorted green
9 fat eighths assorted yellow
$1/2$ yard green fabric for button border
$1 1/2$ yards striped yellow/blue fabric (first and third borders)
$3/4$ yard blue plaid (binding)
4 yards backing
twin-size quilt batting
28 yellow buttons, $3/4$" diameter

Templates
Triangular Log Cabin Patterns, page 51

Cutting
Log Cabin Center Star
1 square, $1 1/2$" x $1 1/2$", blue (A)
1 strip, 1" x $1 1/2$", yellow (B)
2 strips, 1" x 2", yellow (C, D)
1 strip, 1" x $2 1/2$", yellow (E)
1 strip, 1" x $2 1/2$", green (F)
2 strips, 1" x 3", green (G, H)
1 strip, 1" x $3 1/2$", green (I)
1 strip, 1" x $3 1/2$", blue (J)
2 strips, 1" x 4", blue (K, L)
1 strip, 1" x $4 1/2$", blue (M)
4 squares, $2 7/8$" x $2 7/8$", assorted blue (flying geese units)
4 squares, $2 7/8$" x $2 7/8$", assorted yellow (flying geese units)
4 squares, 2" x 2", blue (star corners)
4 strips, 1" x 2", green (star corner logs)
4 strips, 1" x $2 1/2$", green (star corner logs)
4 strips, $1 3/4$"-wide, assorted green fabrics (star border)

Flavin Glover was introduced to the rudiments of quilt making by her mother. After graduating from college and while teaching arts and crafts therapy classes, however, Flavin decided to learn more about quilting in order to enrich her therapeutic classes. Her mother continued to encourage her, and in 1975 a neighbor showed Flavin a beautiful Log Cabin she had hand-pieced and quilted.

Thus began Flavin's thirty year love affair with Log Cabins. She was one of the first to see that the Log Cabin technique could be approached in a variety of ways. She realized that the Log Cabin could become a design foundation that offered versatile pattern options, depth, movement and an opportunity for color play.

Today Flavin Glover's name is almost synonymous with Log Cabin. Her favorite quilt, "Row Houses" which she completed in 1985, was named as one of the "100 Best American Quilts of the 20th Century," out placing over 17,000 quilts that had been considered.

Her quilts and original wearable fashions have been exhibited extensively. She teaches workshops, gives lectures, and still finds time to write books demonstrating her techniques. She and her husband live in the college town of Auburn, Alabama but spend a great deal of time traveling to far-away places where they do humanitarian work.

4. Sort the triangle squares in pairs so that no two pairs are the same. Join triangle squares in pairs to make flying geese unit. (**Diagram 4**) Repeat for three more flying geese units.

Diagram 4

5. For star corner squares, sew 1" x 2" green strip to 2" blue square; sew 1" x 2$^1/2$" green strip to adjacent side. (**Diagram 5**) Repeat for three more star corner squares.

Diagram 5

6. To make Log Cabin Center Star, sew a flying geese unit to opposite sides of center Log Cabin block. (**Diagram 6**)

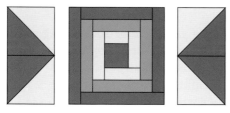

Diagram 6

7. Sew a star corner square to opposite ends of remaining flying geese units. Sew to top and bottom to complete Log Cabin Center Star. (**Diagram 7**)

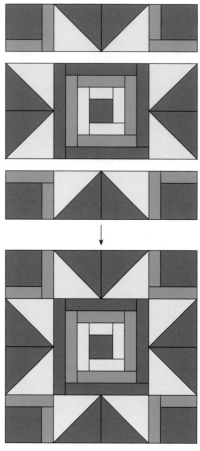

Diagram 7

8. Sew a 1$^3/4$"-wide green strip to one edge of Log Cabin Star Block; cut off excess strip. (**Diagram 8**)

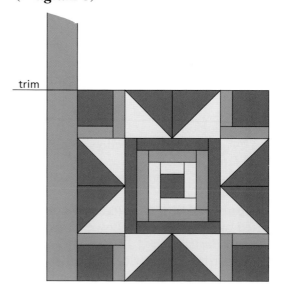

trim

Diagram 8

40

9. Moving clockwise, join another 1³/4"-wide green strip on adjacent side of block; continue until block is bordered. (**Diagram 9**) The block with seams should measure 11" (10¹/2" when finished).

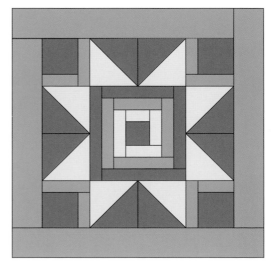

Diagram 9

41

Inner Cornerstones Block

1. Sew a 1¹/4" yellow square (A) to a 1¹/4" blue square (B); sew a 1¹/4" yellow square (A) to a 1¹/4" green square (C). Sew pairs of squares together. (**Diagram 10**)

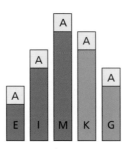

Diagram 10

2. Sew a 1¹/4" yellow square (A) to each of the following: 1¹/4" x 2" blue strip (E), 1¹/4" x 2³/4" green strip (G), 1¹/4" x 3¹/2" blue strip (I), 1¹/4" x 4¹/4" green strip (K) and 1¹/4" x 5" blue strip (M). (**Diagram 11**)

Diagram 11

3. Sew cut strips and pieced strips to center to complete Inner Cornerstones block measuring 5³/4" (5¹/4" finished). (**Diagram 12**) Make seven more Inner Cornerstones blocks.

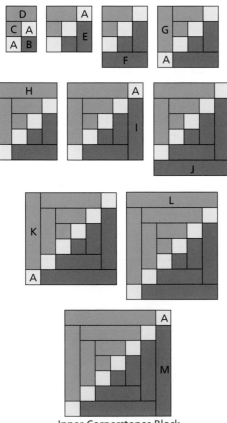

Diagram 12   Inner Cornerstones Block
make 8

Offset Center Block

1. Sew 1" x 1¹/2" yellow strip (B) to 1¹/2" blue square (A); press seam. Sew 1" x 2" yellow strip (C) to adjacent side of A/B. (**Diagram 13**)

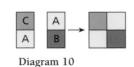

Diagram 13

2. Continue sewing strips alphabetically in same manner until Offset Center block is completed. (**Diagram 14**) Make three more blocks.

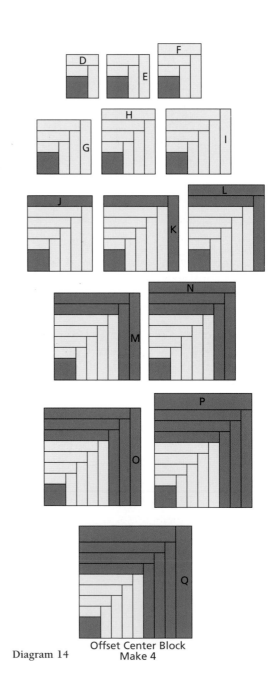

Diagram 14   Offset Center Block
Make 4

42

Making the Quilt Center

1. Arrange the Inner Cornerstones blocks and Offset Center blocks around the Log Cabin Star block. (**Diagram 15**)

Diagram 15

2. Sew two Inner Cornerstones blocks together then sew on one side of the Star block. Repeat for other side. (**Diagram 16**)

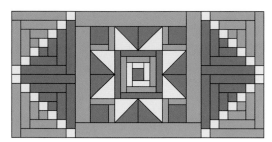

Diagram 16

3. Sew an Offset Center block, two Inner Cornerstones blocks and an Offset Center block in a horizontal line; sew to top of Star block unit. Repeat for bottom of quilt. (**Diagram 17**)

Diagram 17

4. Sew $3^1/2$" x $21^1/2$" green strips to sides of quilt; sew $3^1/2$" x $27^1/2$" green strips to top and bottom. (**Diagram 18**)

Diagram 18

43

Triangular Log Cabin Units

1. Sew a yellow B to a green Triangle A; sew a yellow C to adjacent side, then sew a yellow D to complete first round. (**Diagram 19**)

Diagram 19

2. Continue sewing E through J to complete a Triangle Log Cabin. (**Diagram 20**) Make seven more Triangle Log Cabins with green centers.

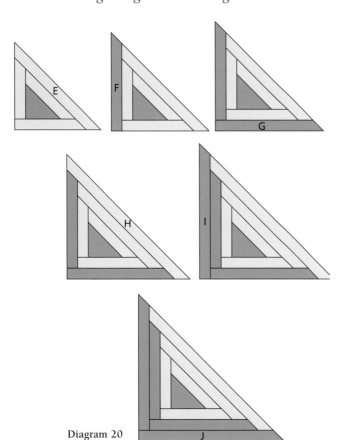

Diagram 20

3. Repeat steps 1 and 2 starting with a yellow Triangle A and using blue and yellow logs, to make eight Triangle Log cabins with yellow centers. (**Diagram 21**)

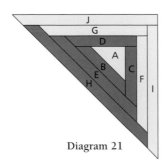

Diagram 21

4. Sew together one of each Triangle Log Cabin to complete Triangular Log Cabin Units. (**Diagram 22**)

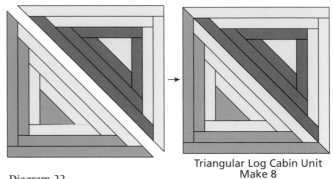

Diagram 22

Triangular Log Cabin Unit
Make 8

Outer Cornerstones Blocks

1. Sew a $1^{1}/4$" yellow square (A) to a $1^{1}/4$" blue square (B); sew a $1^{1}/4$" yellow square (A) to a $1^{1}/4$" green square (C). Sew pairs of squares together. (**Diagram 23**)

Diagram 23

2. Sew a $1^{1}/4$" yellow square (A) to each of the following: $1^{1}/4$" x 2" blue strip (E), $1^{1}/4$" x $2^{3}/4$" green strip (G), $1^{1}/4$" x $3^{1}/2$" blue strip (I), $1^{1}/4$" x $4^{1}/4$" green strip (K), $1^{1}/4$" x 5" blue strip (M), $1^{1}/4$" x $5^{3}/4$" green strip (O), and $1^{1}/4$" x $6^{1}/2$" blue strip (Q). (**Diagram 24**)

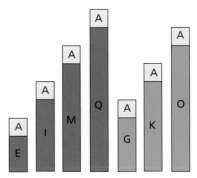

Diagram 24

3. Sew cut strips and pieced strips to center in alphabetical order to complete Inner Cornerstones block measuring $7^{1}/4$" ($6^{3}/4$" finished). (**Diagram 25**) Make 15 more Outer Cornerstones blocks.

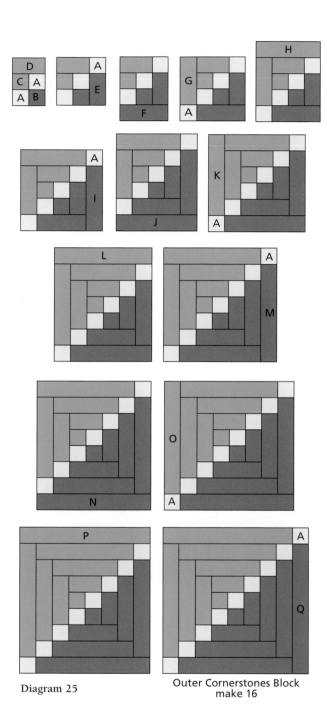

Diagram 27

3. Continue sewing strips in alphabetical order until Rectangular Courthouse Steps block is completed. (**Diagram 28**) Make three more blocks.

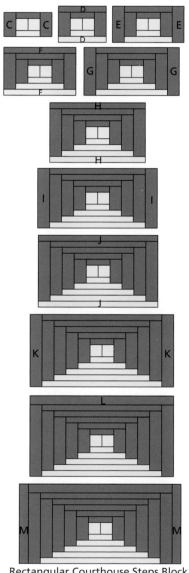

Rectangular Courthouse Steps Block
Make 4

Diagram 28

Diagram 25

Outer Cornerstones Block
make 16

Rectangular Courthouse Steps Blocks

1. Sew two different yellow $1\frac{1}{2}$" squares (A) together. (**Diagram 26**)

Diagram 26

2. Sew a 1" x $2\frac{1}{2}$" blue strip (B) and a 1" x $2\frac{1}{2}$" yellow strip (B) to opposite sides of yellow A/A. (**Diagram 27**)

Offset Center Variation Block

1. Sew a $1^1/2$" x $1^1/2$" green square (B) to a $1^1/2$" x $1^1/2$" blue square (A). Sew to $1^1/2$" x $2^1/2$" green strip (C). Sew a 1" x $2^1/2$" yellow strip (D) and a 1" x 3" yellow strip (E) to complete the first round. (**Diagram 29**)

Diagram 29

2. Continue sewing strips in alphabetical order to complete the Offset Center Variation block. (**Diagram 30**) Make three more blocks.

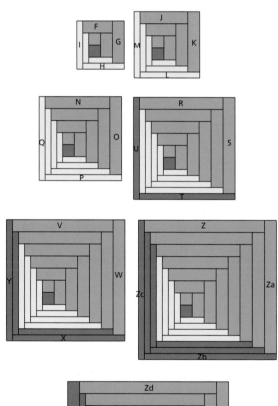

Offset Center Variation Log Cabin
Make 4

Diagram 30

Quilt Assembly

1. Sew two Outer Cornerstones blocks together. Sew a Triangular Log Cabin Units to each end. (**Diagram 31**) Repeat three more times.

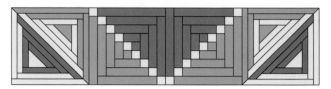

Diagram 31

2. Sew an Outer Cornerstone block to opposite sides of a Rectangular Courthouse Steps Block. (**Diagram 32**)

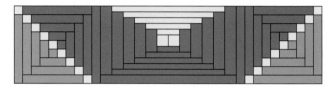

Diagram 32

3. Sew strip from step 1 to strip from step 2. (**Diagram 33**) Repeat three more times.

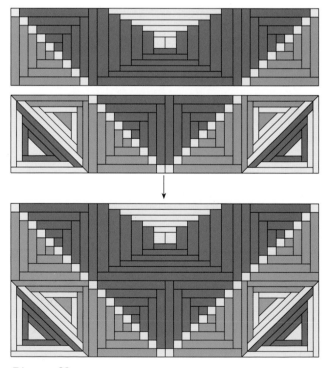

Diagram 33

4. Sew unit from step 3 to opposite sides of quilt center. (**Diagram 34**)

Diagram 34

5. Sew an Offset Variation block to each side of remaining units. Sew to top and bottom of quilt. (**Diagram 35**)

Diagram 35

Finishing

1. For first border, sew $1^1/4$"-wide striped yellow/blue strips in pairs to make four long strips. Refer to Mitered Borders, page 154, to add border.

2. **Note:** *The second border has Nine-Patch and Rail Fence blocks intermingled with random Rail Fence blocks made of leftover strips of various widths. Refer to Quilt Layout to see variations of color and blocks.*

For nine patches, sew a $1^1/2$"-wide blue strip to each side of a $1^1/2$"-wide yellow strip; repeat. Sew a $1^1/2$"-wide yellow strip to each side of a $1^1/2$"-wide blue strip. (**Diagram 36**)

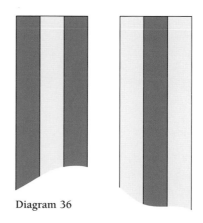

Diagram 36

3. Cut strip sets into $1^1/2$" segments. (**Diagram 37**)

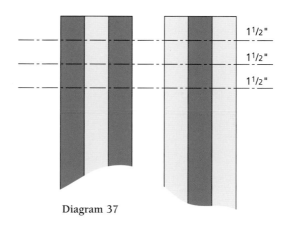

Diagram 37

4. Sew segments together to make nine patch. (**Diagram 38**) Make 22 nine-patch blocks.

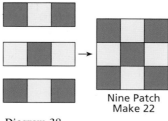

Nine Patch
Make 22

Diagram 38

5. Repeat steps 2 to 4 using green and blue $1^1/2$"-wide strips to make 8 nine-patch blocks. (**Diagram 39**)

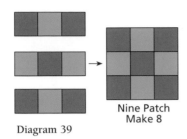

Nine Patch
Make 8

Diagram 39

6. Sew two $1^1/4$" x 22" blue strips and two $1^1/4$" x 22" yellow strips; repeat. Cut into $3^1/2$" segments. Make six rail fence blocks. (**Diagram 40**)

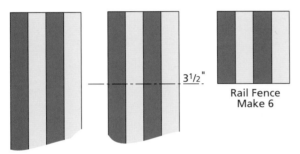

$3^1/2$"

Rail Fence
Make 6

Diagram 40

7. Sew two $1^1/4$" x 22" green strips and two $1^1/4$" x 22" blue strips; repeat. Cut into $3^1/2$" segments. Make six rail fence blocks. (**Diagram 41**)

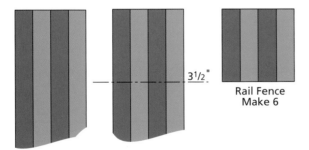

$3^1/2$"

Rail Fence
Make 6

Diagram 41

8. Sew nine patches, rail fence blocks and assorted strips together to make four 56" length strips. (**Diagram 42**)

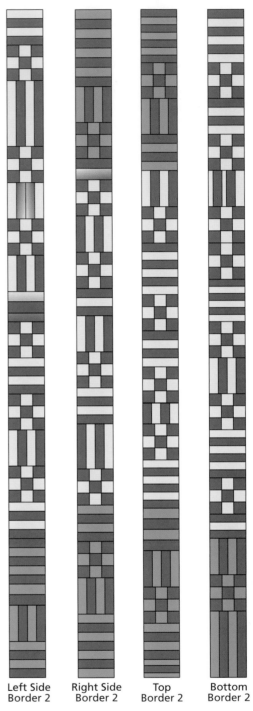

Left Side
Border 2

Right Side
Border 2

Top
Border 2

Bottom
Border 2

Diagram 42

9. Sew border strips to opposite sides of quilt. (**Diagram 43**)

10. Sew a nine patch to each end of remaining border strips and sew to top and bottom of quilt. (**Diagram 44**)

11. For third border, sew 2"-wide border print strips in pairs to make four long strips. Refer to Mitered Borders, page 154, to add border.

12. Refer to Finishing Your Quilt, pages 154 to 159, to complete your quilt.

Optional quilting: A star motif (see pattern on page 50) was quilted in the inner green border. Sew a yellow button in center of each star. Radiating lines were quilted in the Offset Center blocks and the Offset Center Variation blocks. The rest of the quilt was quilted using outline quilting near the ditch of the seams on all blocks and borders.

Mark quilt designs on quilt as shown in Offset Center and Offset Center Variation blocks, as shown. Make a template of Star Button motif to align and mark star designs in the Button Border.

Diagram 43

Diagram 44

49

Spring Star Quilt Layout

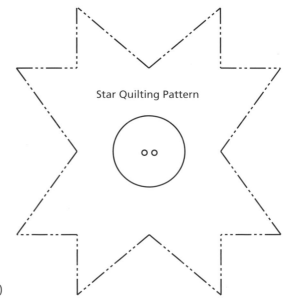

Star Quilting Pattern

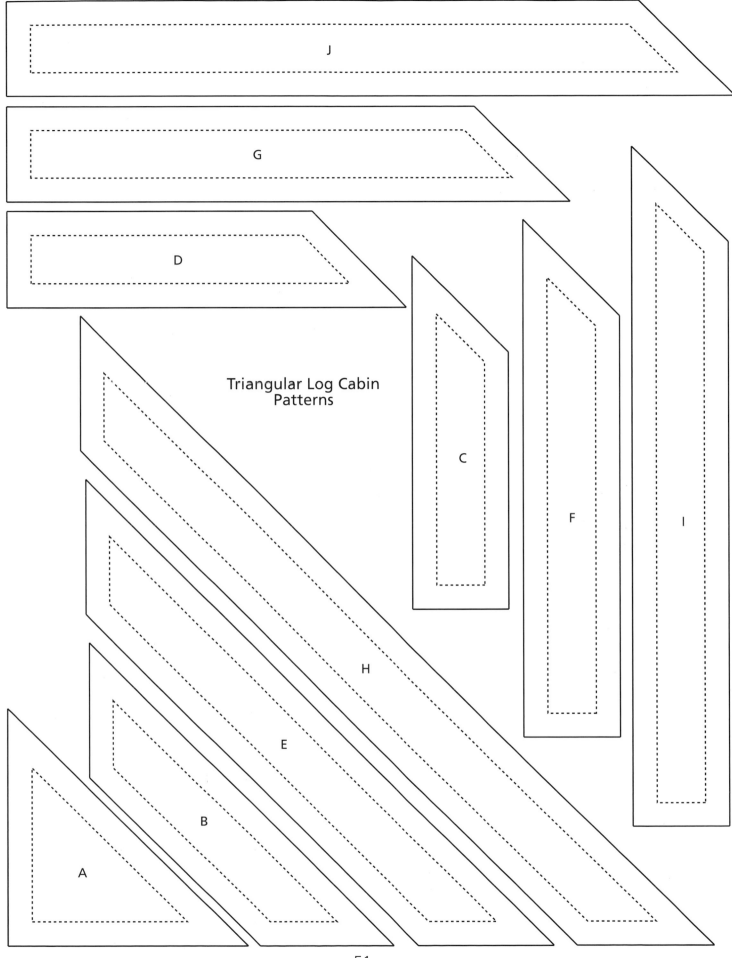

Triangular Log Cabin
Patterns

J

G

D

C

F

I

A

B

E

H

51

A stained glass quilt is actually a pictorial quilt that is intended to resemble stained glass. Colorful Log Cabin blocks filled with picture centers look like stained glass because of the use of bright fabrics and the thin black outlines around the center shapes and logs. Each Log Cabin block holds a different center, and the blocks are separated by different-colored sashing strips with black cornerstones. The entire quilt is foundation pieced.

Stained Glass Log Cabin

by Linda Causee

Approximate Size
31¹/2" x 31¹/2"

Materials
fat quarter each orange, pink, coral, green, blue, purple, yellow, turquoise, red (centers and sashing)
$1/4$ yard light blue
$1/2$ yard medium blue (includes second border)
$1/4$ yard dark blue
$1/4$ yard light pink
$1/4$ yard medium purple
$1/4$ yard dark purple
$1^1/2$ yards black (includes first border, cornerstones and binding)
1 yard backing
batting

Patterns
Square in a Square Center Log Cabin Foundation, page 62
Courthouse Steps Center Log Cabin Foundation, page 57
Flying Geese Center Log Cabin Foundation, page 60
Tulip Center Log Cabin Foundation, page 64
House Center Log Cabin Foundation, page 61
Crazy Center Log Cabin Foundation, page 58
Heart Center Log Cabin Foundation, page 65
Fan Center Log Cabin Foundation, page 59
Triangle Center Log Cabin Foundation, page 63

Linda Causee fell in love with foundation piecing in 1993 when she edited a book which described this technique. Since that time she has been writing books with foundation-pieced designs including among others *365 Foundation Quilt Blocks*, *Symbols of Faith* and *Patchwork for Patriots.*

Linda's expertise at foundation piecing allows her to see this technique in blocks others would not imagine using this technique. She collected a group of them in her book, *24 Blocks You Never Dreamed You Could Paper Piece.*

Because even the smallest pieces meet precisely, quickly and accurately in foundation piecing, it is the perfect venue for miniatures. Here the centers of each of the Log Cabins is another miniature pattern including Square in a Square, Courthouse Steps and Flying Geese.

Cutting

Blocks

Note: *You do not have to cut exact pieces for foundation piecing. However, piecing the outer logs will be easier if you cut strips the widths given below.*

2 strips, 1³/8"-wide, light blue
1 strip, 1³/8"-wide, medium blue
2 strips, 1³/8"-wide, dark blue
3 strips, 1³/8"-wide, light pink
2 strips, 1³/8"-wide, medium purple
2 strips, 1³/8"-wide, dark purple
19 strips, ³/4"-wide, black

Finishing

4 strips, 1¹/2" x 7¹/2", orange (sashing)
4 strips, 1¹/2" x 7¹/2", coral (sashing)
4 strips, 1¹/2" x 7¹/2", pink (sashing)
4 strips, 1¹/2" x 7¹/2", blue (sashing)
4 strips, 1¹/2" x 7¹/2", green (sashing)
4 strips, 1¹/2" x 7¹/2", purple (sashing)
16 squares, 1¹/2" x 1¹/2", black (cornerstones)
4 strips, 1³/4"-wide, black (first border)
4 strips, 2¹/4"-wide, medium blue (second border)
4 strips, 2¹/2"-wide, black

Instructions

Note: *Refer to Foundation Piecing a Log Cabin Block, pages 151 to 154, before beginning.*

1. Make one foundation of each block on pages 57 to 65. (**Diagram 1**)

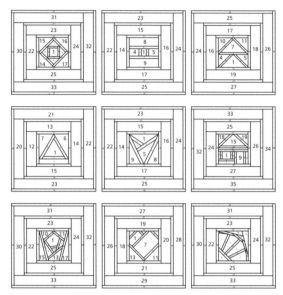

Diagram 1

2. Make blocks using photograph as a guide for color placement of centers. (**Diagram 2**)

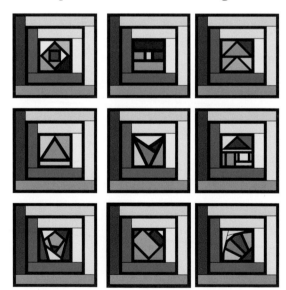

Diagram 2

3. Place blocks in three rows of three blocks with sashing in between. Use the pink, coral and orange sashing strips vertically and the green, blue and purple sashing strips horizontally. (**Diagram 3**)

Diagram 3

4. Sew blocks and vertical sashing strips together in rows. Sew horizontal sashing strips together with 1¹/2" black squares in between and at each end. (**Diagram 4**)

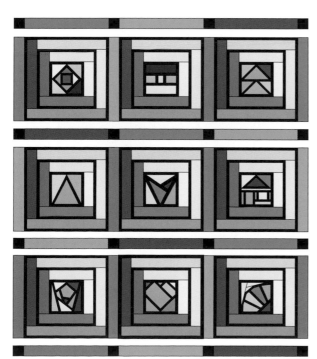

Diagram 4

5. Sew rows together.

6. For first border, measure quilt lengthwise. Cut 1³/4"-wide black strips to that length and sew to sides of quilt. Measure quilt crosswise. Cut 1³/4"-wide black strips to that length and sew to top and bottom of quilt.

7. For second border, repeat step 6 using 2¹/4"-wide medium blue strips.

8. Refer to Finishing Your Quilt, page 154 to 159, to complete your quilt.

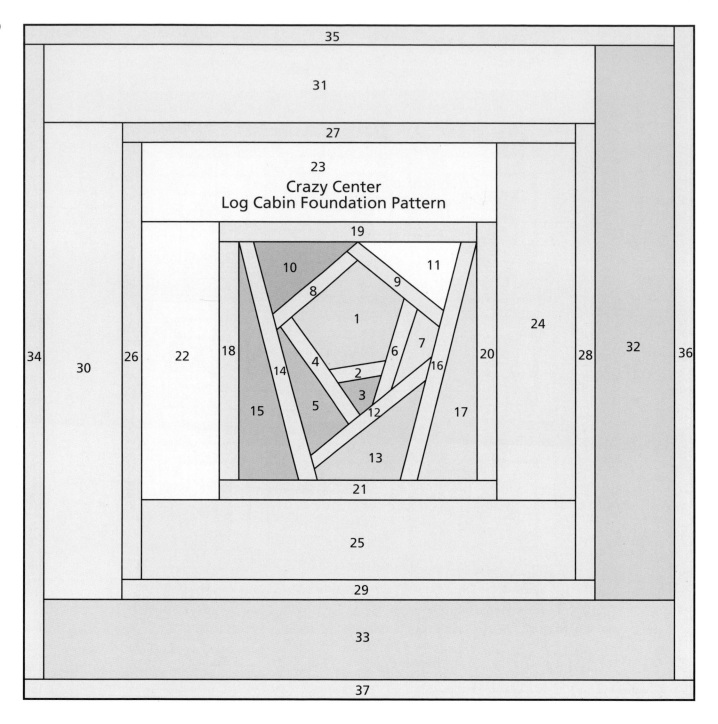

Crazy Center
Log Cabin Foundation Pattern

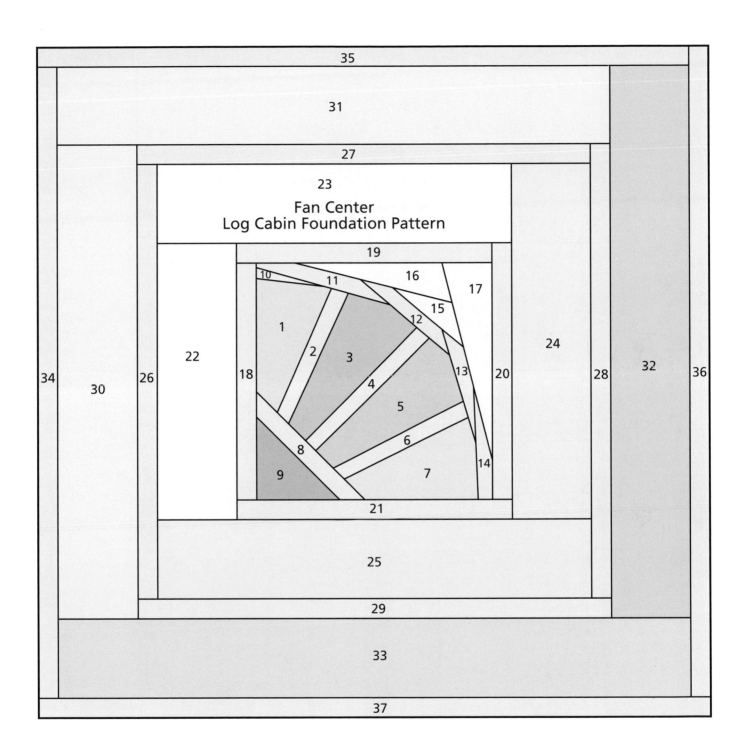

Fan Center
Log Cabin Foundation Pattern

59

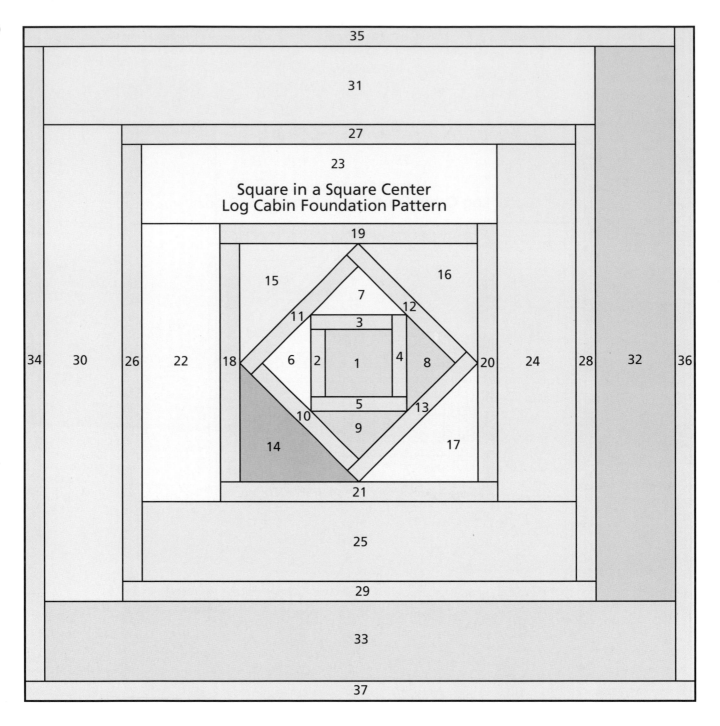

Square in a Square Center
Log Cabin Foundation Pattern

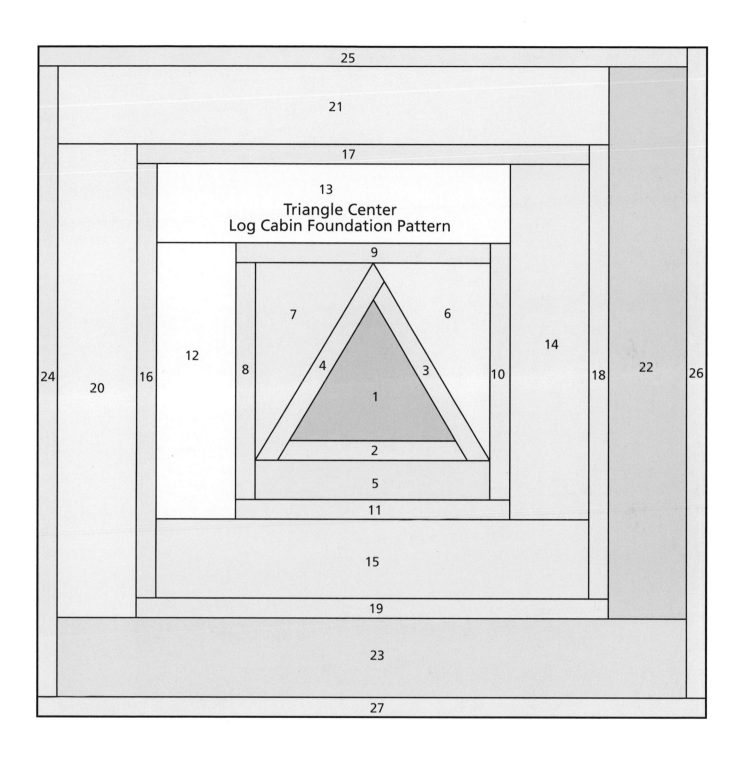

Triangle Center
Log Cabin Foundation Pattern

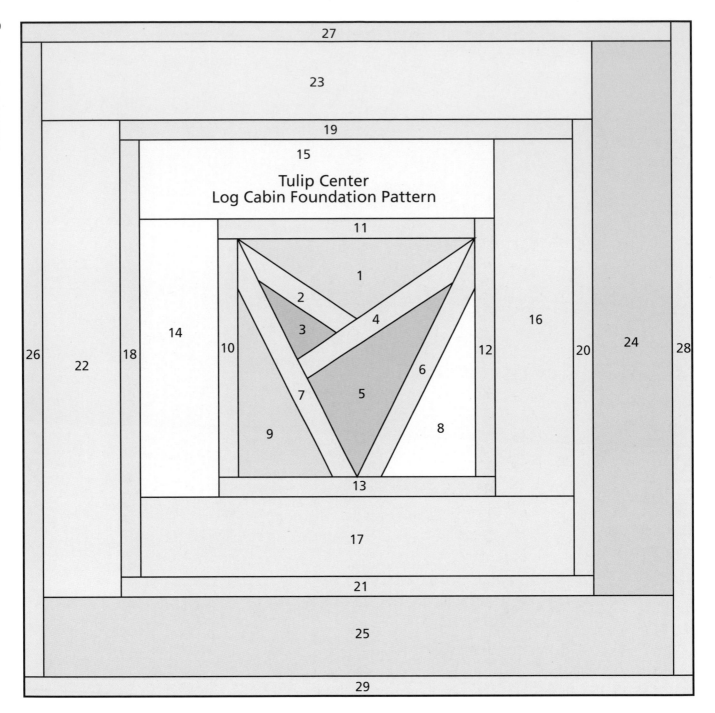

Tulip Center
Log Cabin Foundation Pattern

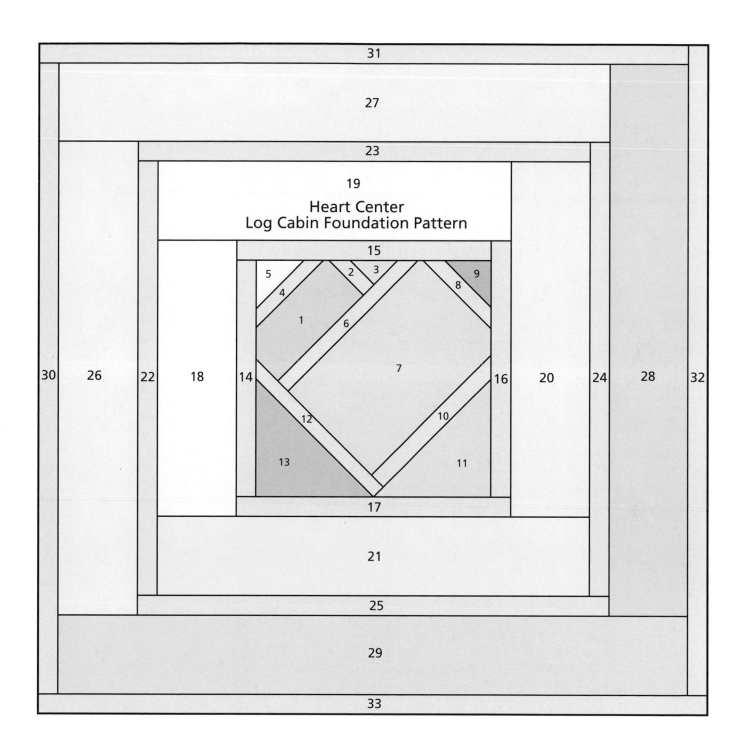

Heart Center
Log Cabin Foundation Pattern

While this may not look like the traditional Log Cabin quilt at first glance, it is actually a Log Cabin. There are 24 Log Cabin blocks, but each block is made with a nine-patch center. The metallic autumn leaf fabric from the Nature's Brilliance collection of Robert Kaufman makes the quilt glow. The use of the nine-patch blocks for the border draws the entire design together.

Logs & Nine Patches

by Christina Jensen

Approximate Size
66" x 87"

Materials
$1^3/8$ yards cream tonal
$7/8$ yard red tonal
$2^3/8$ yards small black print
$1^2/3$ yards gold print
2 yards large leaf print
$5^1/4$ yards backing
batting

Cutting
Blocks
8 strips, 2"-wide, cream tonal (A)
7 strips, $3^1/2$"-wide, cream tonal (C)
2 squares, $3^1/2$" $3^1/2$", cream tonal (L)
11 strips, 2"-wide, red tonal (B)
2 rectangles, 2" x $3^1/2$", red tonal (M)
11 strips, 2"-wide, small black print (D)
    cut 8 strips into 148 squares, 2" x 2" (D)
3 strips, $3^1/2$"-wide, small black print (G)
3 strips, $4^1/4$"-wide, small black print (I)
3 strips, $5^3/4$"-wide, small black print (K)
3 strips, $3^1/2$"-wide, gold print (E)
3 strips, 5"-wide, gold print (F)
3 strips, $4^1/4$"-wide, gold print (H)
3 strips, $5^3/4$"-wide, gold print (J)

Christina Jensen graduated from a prestigious Eastern college with an advanced degree in literature. For years she worked as a writer both in Hollywood and New York.

During that time, Christina was what she calls, "a closet quilter." In her spare time, she made quilts for her friends. It never occurred to her that quilting was a hobby shared by many others. Once Christina retired from her fast-paced work world, she began to explore the quilt world, taking classes wherever she could find them. Before long, Christina had filled her apartment and her life with quilts and quilting friends.

Today, Christina is unhappy if she's not working on at least two quilts at a time. All of her quilts are imaginative and original. She enjoys taking a concept and re-working it as she has done here.

Finishing

6 strips, 2"-wide, small black print (first border)

4 squares, 5" x 5", small black print (cornerstones, second border)

7 strips, 6$^1/2$"-wide, large leaf print (third border)

8 strips, 2$^1/2$"-wide, large leaf print (binding)

Instructions

Blocks

1. Sew 2"-wide cream tonal strip (A) to opposite long sides of 2"-wide red tonal strip (B). Press seams toward B. (**Diagram 1**) Repeat to make four pieced strips.

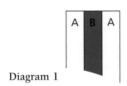

Diagram 1

2. Cut pieced strips into 2" segments. (**Diagram 2**) You will need 72 segments.

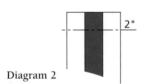

Diagram 2

3. Sew 2"-wide red tonal strip to 3$^1/2$"-wide cream tonal strip (C). Press seam toward B. (**Diagram 3**) Repeat to make seven pieced strips.

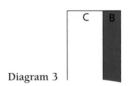

Diagram 3

4. Cut pieced strips into 2" segments. (**Diagram 4**). You will need 144 segments.

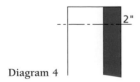

Diagram 4

5. Sew A/B segment between two B/C segments. Press seams toward A/B. (**Diagram 5**) Repeat for 72 units.

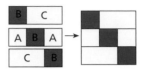

Diagram 5

6. Draw a diagonal line from corner to corner on wrong side of each 2" small black print square (D). (**Diagram 6**)

Diagram 6

7. Place a D square right sides together on the B corners of each pieced unit; stitch on the marked lines. Trim seam allowance to $^1/4$" and press D open to complete nine-patch centers. (**Diagram 7**) Set aside remaining D squares for second border.

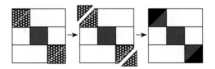

Diagram 7

8. Cut one of each of the following strips in half to make two 21"-22" long half-strips each:
   2"-wide small black print strip (D)
   3$^1/2$"-wide gold print strip (E)
   5"-wide gold print strip (F)
   3$^1/2$"-wide small black print strip (G)
   4$^1/4$"-wide gold print strip (H)
   4$^1/4$"-wide small black print strip (I)
   5$^3/4$"-wide gold print strip (J)
   5$^3/4$"-wide small black print strip (K)

9. Sew a 2"-wide small black print strip (D) to 3$^1/2$"-wide gold print strip (E); press strip toward D. Repeat with D and E half-strips. (**Diagram 8**)

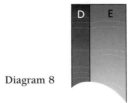

Diagram 8

10. Cut pieced strips into 2" segments. (**Diagram 9**) You will need 24 segments.

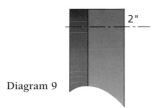

Diagram 9

Diagram 12

11. Sew the following strips and half-strips together then cut into 2" segments for a total of 24 each (**Diagram 10**):

2"-wide small black print (D) and 5" gold print (F)

3$\frac{1}{2}$"-wide gold print strip (E) and 3$\frac{1}{2}$" small black print strip (G)

5"-wide gold print strip (F) and 3$\frac{1}{2}$"-wide small black print strip (G)

4$\frac{1}{4}$"-wide gold print strip (H) and 4$\frac{1}{4}$"-wide small black print strip (I)

4$\frac{1}{4}$"-wide small black print strip (I) and 5$\frac{3}{4}$"-wide gold print (J)

4$\frac{1}{4}$"-wide gold print strip (H) and 5$\frac{3}{4}$"-wide small black print strip (K)

5$\frac{3}{4}$"-wide gold print strip (J) and 5$\frac{3}{4}$"-wide small black print strip (K)

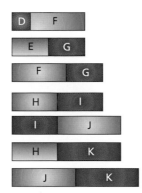

Diagram 10

Press seams toward small black print.

12. Sew a D/E segment to Nine Patch from step 7; press seam toward D/E. Repeat for 24 Nine Patches. (**Diagram 11**) Set aside remaining Nine Patches for border.

Diagram 11

13. Sew a D/F segment to adjacent side of the Nine Patches; press seam toward D/F. (**Diagram 12**)

14. Add E/G and F/G segments to remaining sides of the Nine Patches; press seams toward strips after each addition. (**Diagram 13**)

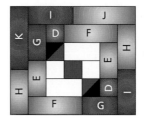

Diagram 13

15. Add final round of segments in the following order to complete 24 blocks: H/I, I/J, H/K, and J/K. (**Diagram 14**)

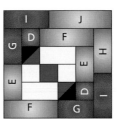

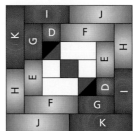

Diagram 14

Finishing

1. Place blocks in six rows of four blocks, turning blocks to offset seams in logs from block to block. (**Diagram 15**)

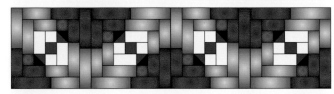

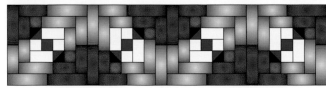

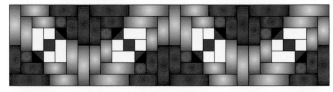

Diagram 15

2. Sew blocks together in rows; press seams for rows in opposite directions. Sew rows together.

3. Measure quilt lengthwise; piece and cut 2"-wide small black print strips to that length. Sew to sides of quilt. Measure quilt crosswise; piece and cut 2"-wide small black print strips to that length. Sew to top and bottom of quilt.

4. Place a 2" small black print square (D) right sides together with a 2" x 3½"red tonal rectangle (M). Sew on marked line, trim seam allowance to ¼" and press D open.

(**Diagram 16**) Repeat on other side of M to complete D/M unit. (**Diagram 17**) Repeat for another D/M unit.

Diagram 16

Make 2

Diagram 17

5. Sew 3½" cream tonal square (L) to D/M unit; repeat. Press seams toward L. (**Diagram 18**)

Diagram 18

6. Sew seven Nine Patches together; repeat. (**Diagram 19**)

Diagram 19

70

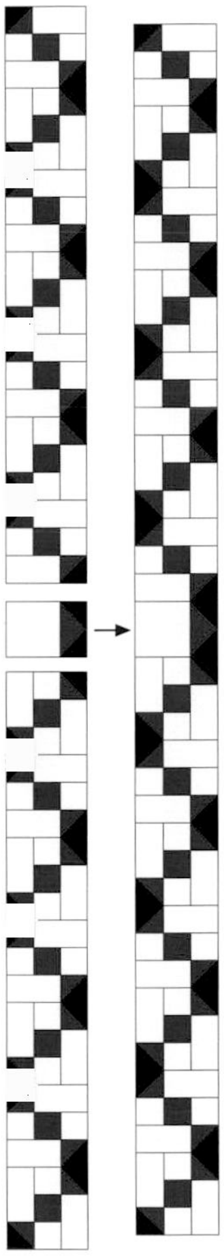

7. Sew Nine Patch strips to opposite side of unit made in step 5. Repeat. (**Diagram 20**)

8. Sew strips to sides of quilt noting position. (**Diagram 21**)

Diagram 20

9. Sew ten Nine Patches together; repeat. Sew a 5" small black print square to each end of each strip. (**Diagram 22**)

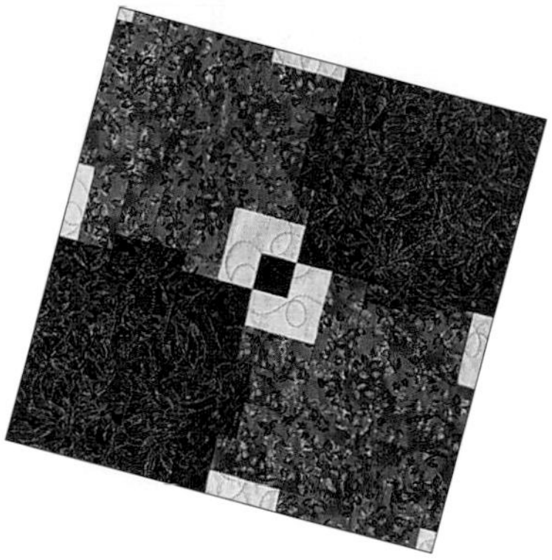

Diagram 21

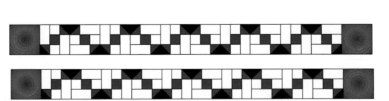

Diagram 22

10. Sew strips to top and bottom of quilt.
    (**Diagram 23**)

Diagram 23

11. Measure quilt lengthwise. Piece and cut $6^{1}/_{2}$"-wide large leaf print strips to that length. Sew to sides of quilt. Measure quilt crosswise. Piece and cut $6^{1}/_{2}$"-wide large leaf print strips to that length. Sew to top and bottom of quilt.

12. Refer to Finishing Your Quilt, pages 154 to 159, to complete your quilt.

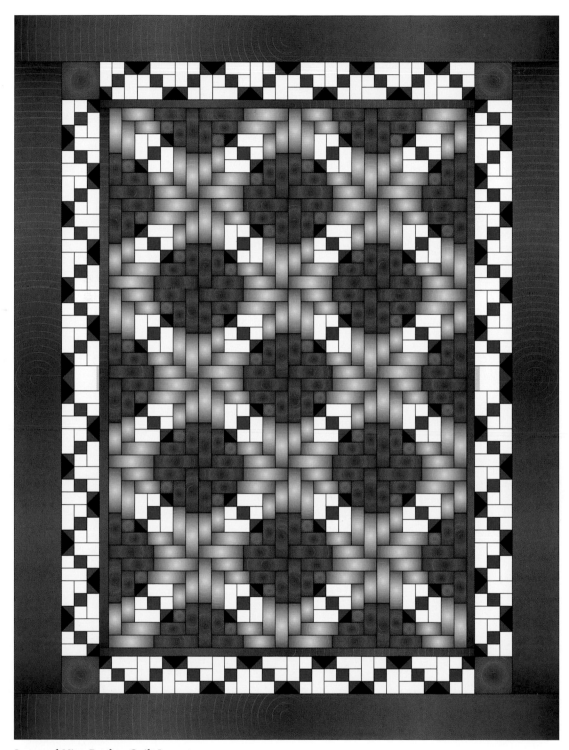

Logs and Nine Patches Quilt Layout

This is a scrap quilt that harkens back to the early days of quilt making when the quilter used every bit of scrap fabric. If a fabric works on the right side, why not use the wrong side as well? In this quilt the blocks are made using both the right and wrong side of all of the fabrics.

Two Sides to Every Story

by Rita Weiss

This quilt uses both the right side and wrong side of all the fabrics.

Approximate Size
34^{1}/2" x 34^{1}/2"

Materials
Note: *The photographed quilt uses assorted scraps, but yardage amounts are given as total amounts needed for light, medium and dark fabrics.*

^{1}/2 yard assorted light blue fabrics
^{3}/8 yard assorted medium blue fabrics
^{3}/8 yard assorted dark blue fabrics
^{1}/2 yard assorted light red fabrics
^{3}/8 yard assorted medium red fabrics
^{3}/8 yard assorted dark red fabrics
^{5}/8 yard dark blue (border and binding)
1^{1}/8 yards backing
batting

Pattern
Log Cabin Foundation Pattern, page 77

Cutting
Blocks
Note: *You do not have to cut exact pieces when foundation piecing. Cut strips in the widths shown below for easier piecing.*

32 squares, 1^{7}/8" x 1^{7}/8", dark red (centers)
7 strips, 1"-wide, dark red (logs 3, 4, 5 and 6)
10 strips, 1"-wide, medium red (logs 7, 8, 9 and 10)

Necessity was the force that pushed **Rita Weiss** into the quilting world. She was working as a junior editor for a New York publisher when a quilting book came across her desk. Because she was the only woman in the editorial department, it was assumed that she knew how to quilt. Rather than admit defeat, Rita immediately scanned every book then available on quilting and taught herself to quilt.

Thirty years later, she is still enchanted by the quilt world. She has written several quilt books including *Quilts in a Hurry*, *Making Antique Quilts* and *Winning Quilts.* In addition Rita served on the board of the International Quilt Association for two terms including one as president.

She has taught and lectured on quilts all over the world and has been called upon to judge competitions.

13 strips, 1"-wide, light red (logs 11, 12, 13 and 14)
32 squares, 1⅞" x 1⅞", dark blue (centers)
7 strips, 1"-wide, dark blue (logs 3, 4, 5 and 6)
10 strips, 1"-wide medium blue (logs 7, 8, 9 and 10)
13 strips, 1"-wide light blue (logs 11, 12, 13 and 14)

Finishing

2 strips, 1½" x 32½", dark blue (border)
2 strips, 1½" x 34½", dark blue (border)
4 strips, 2½"-wide, dark blue (binding)

Instructions

1. Make 64 Log Cabin foundations referring to Preparing the Foundation, page 151. (**Diagram 1**)

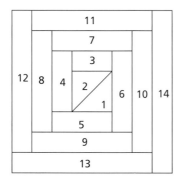

Diagram 1

2. Make four Log Cabin blocks with all "wrong-side" red logs, 28 Log Cabin blocks with "wrong-side" and "right-side" red logs, and 32 Log Cabin blocks with "wrong-side" and "right-side" blue logs. (**Diagram 2**)

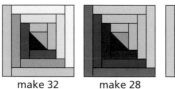

make 32   make 28   make 4

Diagram 2

Piecing Note: *For each block, choose a dark square, light strip, medium strip and dark strip. Cut the square in half. Use the triangle wrong side up for space 1 and the triangle right side up for space 2. Use the dark strip, wrong side up for spaces 3 and 4; use the dark strip, right side up for spaces 5 and 6. Place the medium strip wrong side up on spaces 7 and 8; place right side up on spaces 9 and 10. Finally, use the dark strip wrong side up on spaces 11 and 12; use right side up on spaces 13 and 14.*

3. Place the blocks in eight rows of eight blocks referring to **Diagram 3**. Sew together in rows then sew rows together.

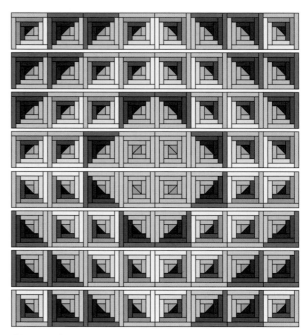

Diagram 3

4. Sew 1½" x 32½" dark blue strips to sides of quilt; press seams toward border. Sew 1½" x 34½" dark blue strips to top and bottom of quilt; press seams toward border.

5. Refer to Finishing Your Quilt, pages 154 to 159, to complete your quilt.

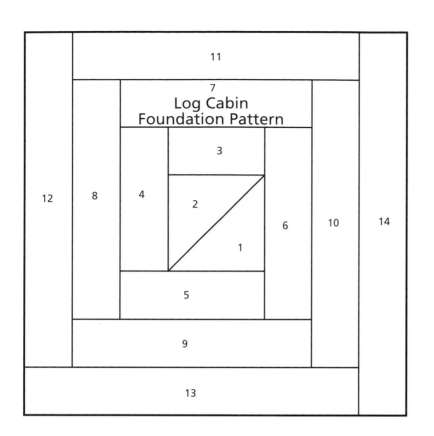

Log Cabin
Foundation Pattern

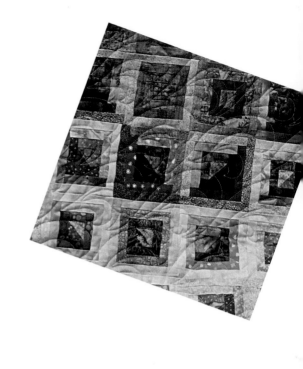

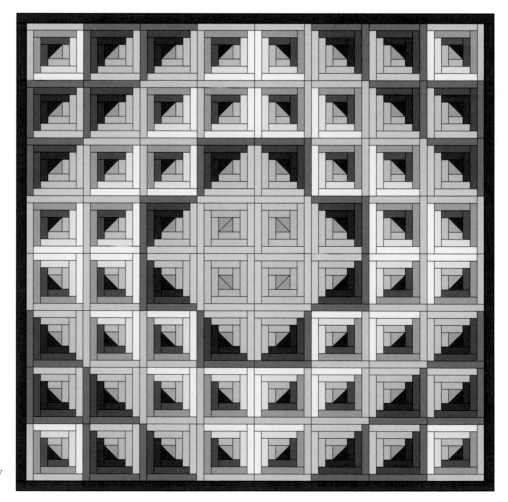

Two Sides to Every Story
Quilt Layout

Take advantage of printed fabric pictures to establish a theme for your Log Cabin Quilt. Can you imagine a fly fisherman who wouldn't love to receive this quilt? Marti used 11 of the 15 available animal designs in this particular fabric. At least 35 other fabrics were used for the strips. The blocks are in three sections: those in the top two rows become sky and are shades of blue. The bottom rows are dark to simulate earth.

Gone Fishin'

by Marti Michell

Approximate Size
$67^1/2$" x $79^1/2$"

Materials
$1^1/2$ yards outdoors novelty print (You may need more or
    less fabric depending on the novelty print used.)
$1^1/4$ yard assorted light tan fabrics
$1/3$ yard assorted medium tan fabrics
$1/2$ yard assorted dark tan fabrics
1 yard assorted light blue fabrics
$1^1/4$ yards assorted green fabrics
1 yard medium blue (border and binding)
1 yard dark green (border and binding)
$4^3/4$ yards backing
batting

Cutting
Notes: *Follow the cutting instructions below or use the wonderful new tool by Marti Michell called My Favorite Log Cabin Ruler. See more about this tool on page 84. Marti finds the easiest way to make a quilt like this is to cut bunches of strips to the correct lengths needed for the block and then arrange them on a design wall. Any leftover strips just go into the box of 2" strips for scrap quilts.*

Block A1
5 squares, $3^1/2$" x $3^1/2$", dark tan (centers)
5 strips, 2" x $3^1/2$", light tan (log 1)
5 strips, 2" x 5", light tan (log 2)
5 strips, 2" x 5", light blue (log 3)
5 strips, 2" x $6^1/2$", light blue (log 4)
5 strips, 2" x $6^1/2$", light tan (log 5)
5 strips, 2" x 8", light tan (log 6)
5 strips, 2" x 8", light blue (log 7)

Marti Michell's mom taught her to sew, and she was an active member of 4-H in high school, which may have influenced her decision to major in Textiles and Home Ec Journalism at Iowa State University, where she met her husband Dick.

Soon after the birth of her two children, Marti started teaching sewing in her home. Eventually the simple sewing instructions turned to quilting lessons, and she was on her way. Marti and Dick began *Yours Truly,* one of the first companies to sell a complete line of quilting supplies including fabric, batting, books and notions.

Yours Truly was sold in 1986, and Marti began free lancing: designing fabrics and writing books. About 10 years ago, Marti and Dick began their *From Marti Michell* company (www.frommarti.com) which manufactures and sells their Perfect Patchwork Templates, a variety of tools, and Marti's self-published books. This Log Cabin quilt is a wonderful representation of that company. Their Log Cabin Rulers were used to cut the strips, and the quilt, assembled in three sections for easy machine quilting, was completed following Marti's book, *Easy Machine Quilting in Sections.*

In 2004, Marti was honored by the International Quilt Festival as the winner of the coveted Silver Star Award for her important and lasting contributions to quilting.

5 strips, 2" x 9^1/$_2$", light blue (log 8)
5 strips, 2" x 9^1/$_2$", light tan (log 9)
5 strips, 2" x 11", light tan (log 10)
5 strips, 2" x 11", light blue (log 11)
5 strips, 2" x 12^1/$_2$", light blue (log 12)

Block A2

2 squares, 3^1/$_2$" x 3^1/$_2$", dark tan (centers)
2 strips, 2" x 3^1/$_2$", medium tan (log 1)
2 strips, 2" x 5", medium tan (log 2)
2 strips, 2" x 5", green (log 3)
2 strips, 2" x 6^1/$_2$", green (log 4)
2 strips, 2" x 6^1/$_2$", medium tan (log 5)
2 strips, 2" x 8", medium tan (log 6)
2 strips, 2" x 8", green (log 7)
2 strips, 2" x 9^1/$_2$", green (log 8)
2 strips, 2" x 9^1/$_2$", medium tan (log 9)
2 strips, 2" x 11", medium tan (log 10)
2 strips, 2" x 11", green (log 11)
2 strips, 2" x 12^1/$_2$", green (log 12)

Block A3

1 square, 3^1/$_2$" x 3^1/$_2$", dark tan (centers)
1 strip, 2" x 3^1/$_2$", light tan (log 1)
1 strip, 2" x 5", light tan (log 2)
1 strip, 2" x 5", medium blue (log 3)
1 strip, 2" x 6^1/$_2$", medium blue (log 4)
1 strip, 2" x 6^1/$_2$", light tan (log 5)
1 strip, 2" x 8", light tan (log 6)
1 strip, 2" x 8", medium blue (log 7)
1 strip, 2" x 9^1/$_2$", medium blue (log 8)
1 strip, 2" x 9^1/$_2$", light tan (log 9)
1 strip, 2" x 11", light tan (log 10)
1 strip, 2" x 11", medium blue (log 11)
1 strip, 2" x 12^1/$_2$", medium blue (log 12)

Block A4

4 squares, 3^1/$_2$" x 3^1/$_2$", dark tan (centers)
4 strips, 2" x 3^1/$_2$", dark tan (log 1)
4 strips, 2" x 5", dark tan (log 2)
4 strips, 2" x 5", green (log 3)
4 strips, 2" x 6^1/$_2$", green (log 4)
4 strips, 2" x 6^1/$_2$", dark tan (log 5)
4 strips, 2" x 8", dark tan (log 6)
4 strips, 2" x 8", green (log 7)
4 strips, 2" x 9^1/$_2$", green (log 8)
4 strips, 2" x 9^1/$_2$", dark tan (log 9)
4 strips, 2" x 11", dark tan (log 10)
4 strips, 2" x 11", green (log 11)
4 strips, 2" x 12^1/$_2$", green (log 12)

Block B1

5 squares, 6^1/$_2$" x 6^1/$_2$", novelty print (centers)
5 strips, 2" x 6^1/$_2$", light tan (log 1)
5 strips, 2" x 8", light tan (log 2)
5 strips, 2" x 8", light blue (log 3)
5 strips, 2" x 9^1/$_2$", light blue (log 4)
5 strips, 2" x 9^1/$_2$", light tan (log 5)
5 strips, 2" x 11", light tan (log 6)
5 strips, 2" x 11", light blue (log 7)
5 strips, 2" x 12^1/$_2$", light blue (log 8)

Block B2

5 squares, 6^1/$_2$" x 6^1/$_2$", novelty print (centers)
5 strips, 2" x 6^1/$_2$", light tan (log 1)
5 strips, 2" x 8", light tan (log 2)
5 strips, 2" x 8", green (log 3)
5 strips, 2" x 9^1/$_2$", green (log 4)
5 strips, 2" x 9^1/$_2$", light tan (log 5)
5 strips, 2" x 11", light tan (log 6)
5 strips, 2" x 11", green (log 7)
5 strips, 2" x 12^1/$_2$", green (log 8)

Block B3

5 squares, 6^1/$_2$" x 6^1/$_2$", novelty print (centers)
5 strips, 2" x 6^1/$_2$", dark tan (log 1)
5 strips, 2" x 8", dark tan (log 2)
5 strips, 2" x 8", green (log 3)
5 strips, 2" x 9^1/$_2$", green (log 4)
5 strips, 2" x 9^1/$_2$", dark tan (log 5)
5 strips, 2" x 11", dark tan (log 6)
5 strips, 2" x 11", green (log 7)
5 strips, 2" x 12^1/$_2$", green (log 8)

Finishing

1 rectangle, 24^1/$_2$" x 36^1/$_2$", novelty print (center)
4 strips, 3^3/$_4$"-wide, medium blue (border)
4 strips, 3^3/$_4$"-wide, dark green (border)
4 strips, 2^1/$_2$"-wide, medium blue (binding)
4 strips, 2^1/$_2$"-wide, dark green (binding)

Instructions

1. Referring to Making a Log Cabin Block, pages 146 to 147, make Log Cabin blocks in the following colors and amounts. (**Diagram 1**) **Note:** *Since the 6¹/2" centers of the Log Cabin blocks are directional, you need to be sure that the first strip is on the left side of the motif as you face the quilt. Add strips clockwise.*

2. Place blocks in rows with 24¹/2" x 36¹/2" outdoors novelty print rectangle. (**Diagram 2**)

3. Sew together blocks for rows 1, 5 and 6. (**Diagram 3**)

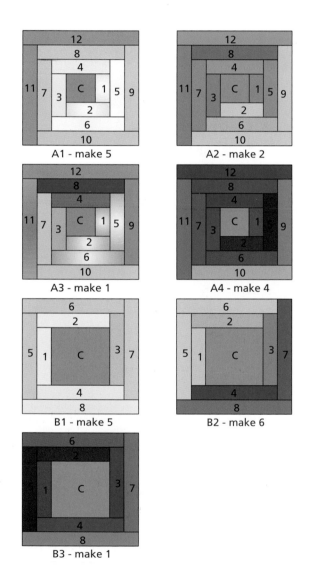

A1 - make 5

A2 - make 2

A3 - make 1

A4 - make 4

B1 - make 5

B2 - make 6

B3 - make 1

Diagram 1

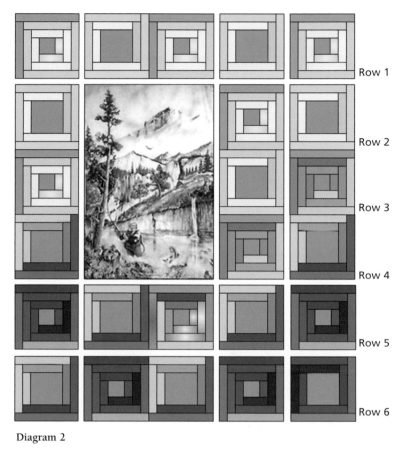

Row 1

Row 2

Row 3

Row 4

Row 5

Row 6

Diagram 2

Row 1

Row 5

Row 6

Diagram 3

4. Sew together three vertical blocks to the left of outdoors novelty print rectangle. Sew to rectangle. (**Diagram 4**)

Diagram 4

5. Sew together pairs of blocks in rows 2, 3 and 4. Sew pairs together then sew to right edge of outdoors novelty print rectangle. (**Diagram 5**)

Diagram 5

6. Sew rows together. (**Diagram 6**)

7. Measure quilt lengthwise. Sew 3³/4"-wide medium blue and dark green strip together diagonally and trim to measured length; repeat. Sew strips to sides of quilt matching diagonal seam of border with the "sky" and "earth" theme of the quilt. (**Diagram 7**)

8. Measure quilt crosswise; piece and cut 3³/4"-wide medium blue strips to that length. Sew to top of quilt. Repeat with 3³/4"-wide dark green strips and sew to bottom of quilt. (**Diagram 8**)

Diagram 6

Diagram 7

9. Refer to Finishing Your Quilt, pages 154 to 159, to complete your quilt. For easier machine quilting, Marti Michell chose to finish this quilt in sections according to the instructions in her book, *Easy Machine Quilting in Sections*.

Diagram 8

Optional:

Cutting with My Favorite Log Cabin Ruler

1. Open the fabric and fold it crosswise on your cutting mat so that the fold line is closest to you and the selvage is along the right edge. Line up a horizontal line on a standard acrylic ruler with the fold line and trim away the selvage. (**Diagram A**)

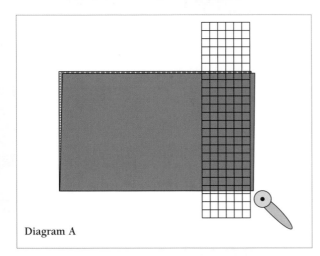

Diagram A

2. The strip width is measured from the right. Working with the 2" strip width (cut), align the appropriate vertical line on the Log Cabin Ruler with the newly-cut straight edge of fabric. (**Diagram B**)

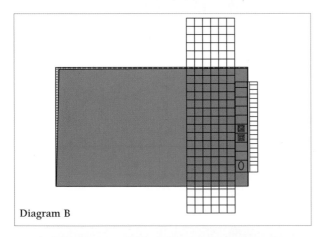

Diagram B

3. Hold the Log Cabin Ruler in place and bring a standard 6" x 24" acrylic ruler into position along the left side of the Log Cabin Ruler. Remove the Log Cabin Ruler and cut along the edge of the standard ruler.

(**Diagram C**) **Note:** *You are not using the standard ruler to measure; it is just a convenient cutting edge.*

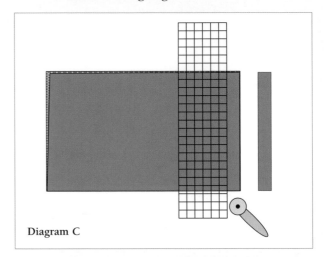

Diagram C

4. Lift the strips; do not remove the ruler yet. When you measure and cut from the right, you can move the strips and confirm that all the threads are cut before you move the standard ruler.

Note: *Stack as many strips as you can cut at one time, or as many as you need for your project.*

5. Now it's time to cut strips to length. With the Log Cabin Ruler extending to the left and the strip length extending to the right, measure and cut the number of center squares or logs needed. **(Diagram D) Note:** *The Log Cabin Ruler is marked with both a letter and the actual length in inches for each strip (log)—just the lines you need, so there's not distraction, no confusion, with unnecessary information.*

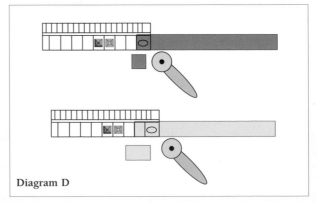

Diagram D

Gone Fishin' Quilt Layout

One of the glories of the Log Cabin is its ability to transform itself into many different guises. This quilt and the quilt on page 94 become photos of a city. Here is the Chicago skyline with the Sears Tower on the left and the Hancock building on the right. Lake Michigan is represented by the blue blocks in the foreground. Various styles of Log Cabin blocks are foundation-pieced to make up this small quilt or wall hanging.

Chicago Skyline
by Linda Causee

Approximate Size
26" x 30"

Materials
1 yard black 1 (Sears Tower building, second border, binding)
$1/4$ yard black 2 (Hancock building)
$1/8$ yard black/white (buildings)
$1/4$ yard dark gray (buildings)
$1/4$ yard light gray (buildings)
$3/8$ yard medium peach (buildings, first border)
$1/8$ yard light peach (buildings)
$1/2$ yard very light blue (sky)
$1/4$ yard light blue (sky)
$1/8$ yard medium blue (water)
$1/8$ yard dark blue (water)
$1/8$ yard dark aqua (water)
$1/8$ yard light green (shrubs)
$1/8$ yard yellow green (shrubs)
$1/8$ yard medium green (shrubs)
1 yard backing
batting

Patterns
Log Cabin Foundation Patterns A - DD, pages 91 to 93

Cutting
Note: *You do not have to cut exact pieces when foundation piecing, but you can cut strips in the widths shown below for easier piecing.*

Blocks
3 strips, 1"-wide, black 1 (logs, Sears Tower building)
1 strip, $1^1/2$"-wide, black 1 (centers, Sears Tower building)
3 strips, 1"-wide, black 2 (logs, Hancock building)
1 strip, $1^1/2$"-wide, black 2 (centers, Hancock building)

Linda Causee spent her early life in the Chicago area but moved to California when she was very young. She often returned to the city to work during her summer vacations from college.

Although Linda majored in science in college, she has "majored" in quilt making for most of her life. For many years she worked as the quilt editor for a major needlework publishing company. Recently she has begun to free lance, writing quilting books on her own.

Linda lives in Oceanside, California with her husband of 25 years, Rick. Her son, Christopher, is a Lieutenant Junior Grade in the United States Navy and her daughter, Kathryn, is a sophmore college student. Angel, the family's adored pug, is the only child who lives at home.

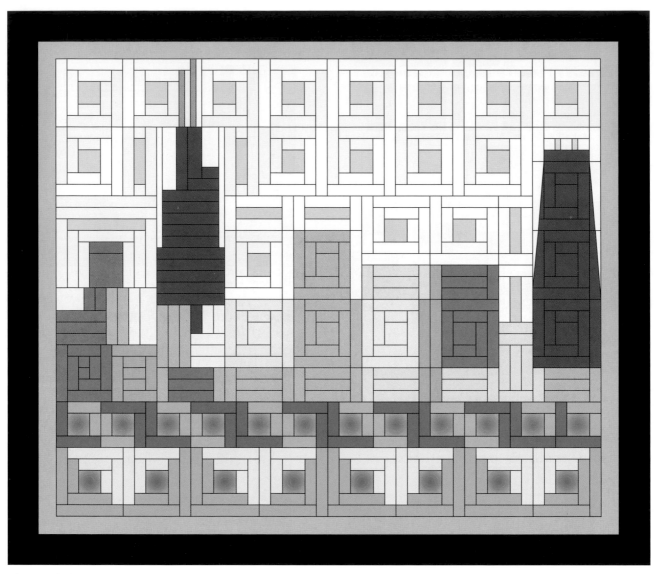

Chicago Skyline Quilt Layout

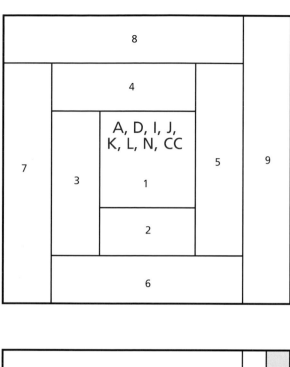

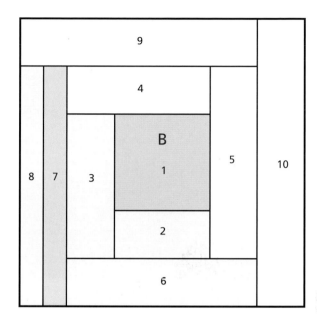

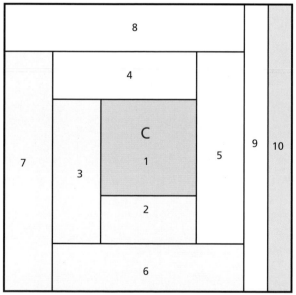

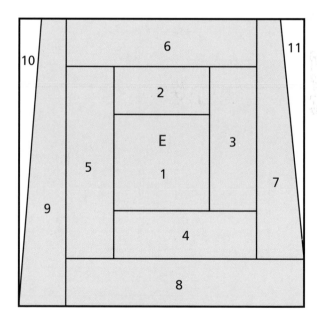

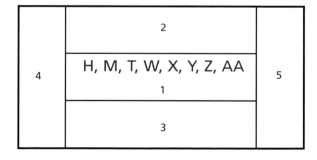

Chicago Skyline
Foundation Patterns

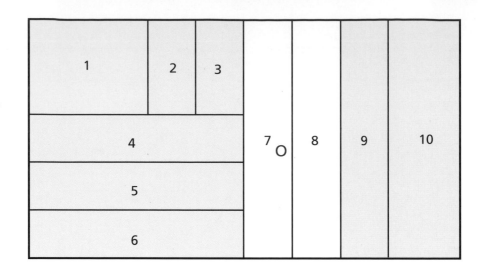

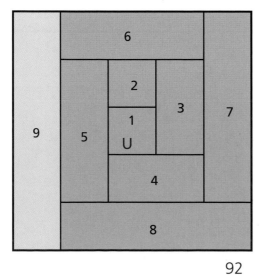

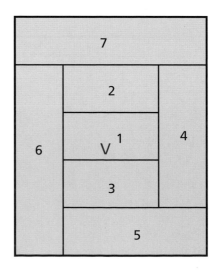

92

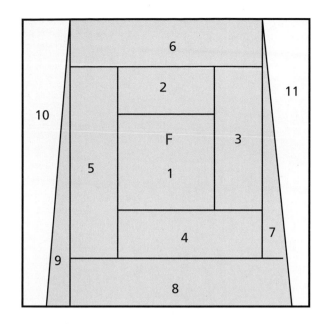

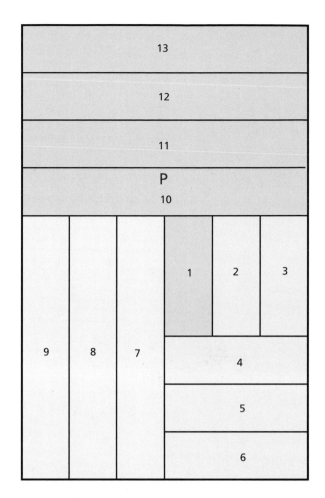

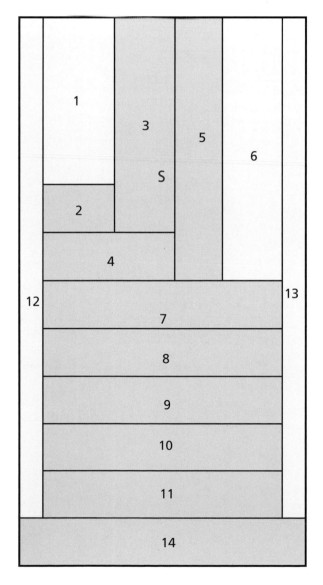

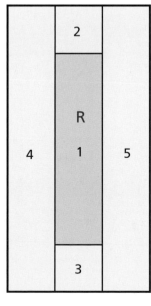

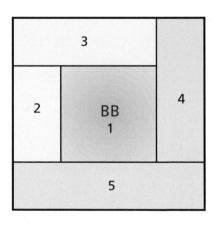

Chicago Skyline
Foundation Patterns

93

Like the Chicago Skyline on page 86, the New York skyline is created here from Log Cabin blocks. The Statue of Liberty stands watch over New York. The Twin Towers are not really there, but their presence is still felt, and if you look closely at the quilt, you can see them between the other buildings. The light blue fabric used for the sky is reversed and indicates where the towers once stood. Straight lines were then quilted vertically through the Tower blocks.

New York Remembered

by Linda Causee

Approximate Size
30" x 30"

Materials
scrap black (buildings)
scrap black/white (buildings)
$1/8$ yard medium gray (buildings)
$1/4$ yard light gray (buildings)
scrap peach (buildings)
$5/8$ yard light blue (sky)
$1/4$ yard dark aqua (water)
scrap light green floral (island)
$1/8$ yard medium green leaf (island)
$1/4$ yard yellow green (Statue of Liberty, first border)
$5/8$ yard black (second border, binding)
1 yard backing
batting

Patterns
Log Cabin Foundation Patterns, pages, 98, 100, 101

Cutting
Note: *You do not have to cut exact pieces when foundation piecing. Cut strips in the widths shown below for easier piecing of logs. Center squares are cut $1^1/2$".*

Blocks
1 strip, $1^1/4$"-wide, black (buildings logs)
1 strip, $1^1/4$"-wide, black/white (buildings logs)
2 strips, $1^1/4$"-wide, medium gray (buildings logs)
2 strips, $1^1/4$"-wide, light gray (buildings logs)
1 strip, $1^1/4$"-wide, peach (building logs)
1 strip, $1^1/2$"-wide, light blue (sky centers)

Linda Causee once again uses her love of foundation piecing to create another version of the Log Cabin, a quilt block that Linda has explored since 1992. She estimates that she has made over 500 different Log Cabin blocks.

Although Linda has a degree in science from the University of California, today she applies her science background to manipulating the various intricate quilt squares.

Linda's favorite method of quilt making is foundation piecing. Although she makes use of other techniques, foundation piecing remains her favorite because it is fast and always accurate, a little bit like painting by numbers with fabric.

This mother of two was for many years the quilt editor of a needle-work publisher. She resigned several years ago and now devotes herself to accepting quilt challenges that she enjoys, as exemplified by this quilt.

New York Remembered
Foundation Patterns
Pattern Note:
All but two of the Foundation patterns are used for more than one block depending on the fabric placements of the logs. Follow the instructions and numbering in red where noted to add extra pieces to the block. For example, follow the numbering in black for blocks D, E, F, I, J, K, R, and S. For block B, add the line where noted in red and change the numbering sequence as noted with red.

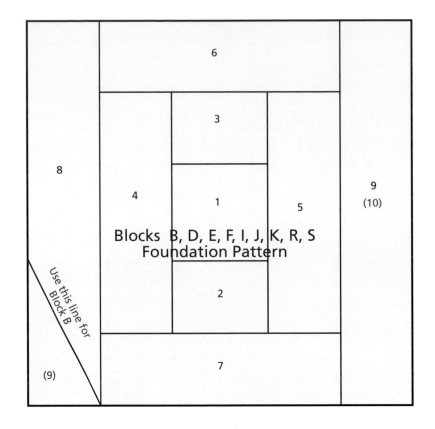

Blocks B, D, E, F, I, J, K, R, S
Foundation Pattern

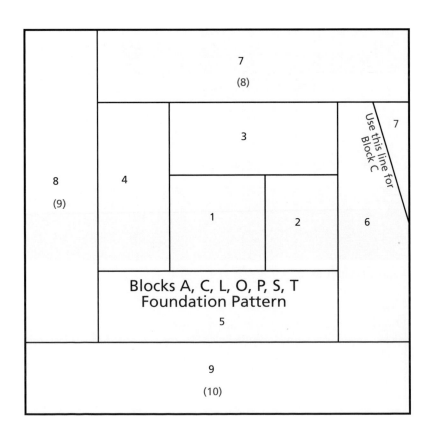

Blocks A, C, L, O, P, S, T
Foundation Pattern

100

New York Remembered
Foundation Patterns
Pattern Note:
All but two of the Foundation patterns are used for more than one block depending on the fabric placements of the logs. Follow the instructions and numbering in red where noted to add extra pieces to the block. For example, follow the numbering in black for blocks D, E, F, I, J, K, R, and S. For block B, add the line where noted in red and change the numbering sequence as noted with red.

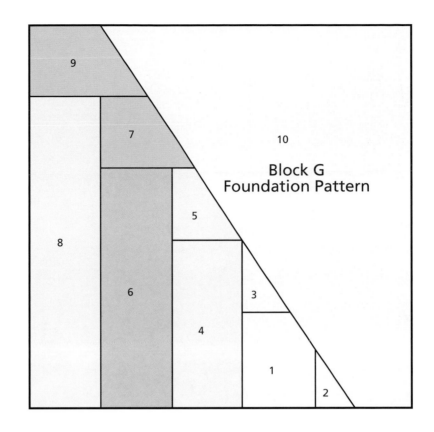

Block G
Foundation Pattern

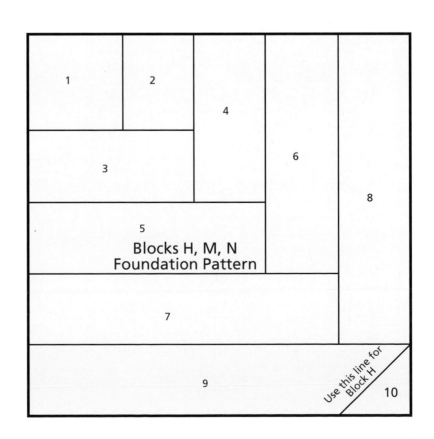

Blocks H, M, N
Foundation Pattern

Use this line for Block H

Log cabin quilts don't always have to be square! In this design a 60 degree diamond is the center of the block. Careful attention must be given when trimming each log addition. While this quilt was made using the Easy Six™ ruler, strips can be cut with a rotary cutter and an acrylic ruler and sewn to the diamond center. This quilt can be as large or small as you wish to make it. A great way to use your treasured stash!

Log Cabin Cubes

By Sharon Hultgren

Approximate Size
37¹/₂" x 41¹/₂"

Materials
6 fat quarters each light, medium and dark fabrics
1 yard backing
batting

Tool/Template
Easy Six™ available from EZ Quilting by Wrights
Optional Diamond Template, page 107

Cutting
Note: *If using the Easy Six™ tool, see Instructions below for cutting. Otherwise, cut the following from fat quarters.*

10 Diamonds each, light, medium and dark fabrics
1¹/₂"-wide strips, light, medium and dark fabrics

Instructions

Note: *The following instructions are for using the Easy Six™. If you do not have an Easy Six™ tool, start with step 5 on page 104 and use your acrylic ruler to trim strips.*

1. Fold a fat quarter in half bringing the selvage edge to the cut, center edge. Straighten the bottom edge of the fabric. Place the Easy Six™ on the bottom edge of the fabric. Note the 2¹/₂" finished line. Cut across the fabric. (**Diagram 1**)

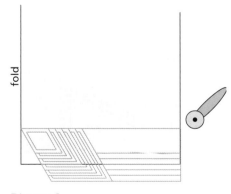

Diagram 1

Sharon Hultgren has been in the quilting industry for the past 18 years, and she understands the time, care and energy that goes into each and every quilting project.

She owned her own quilt shop for four years, and she enjoyed the uplifting experience inherent in the quilting industry. As both Sharon and the industry grew, she created a series of quilting accessories for EZ Quilting to simplify projects including the Easy Six™ used to make this quilt. In addition, she has written a number of books, created many products to assist in the quilting process and taught quilting classes throughout the country and overseas. Recently she joined with Airtex to design "Roll and Quilt", a product that is perfect for panel quilts.

Sharon lives in northern Minnesota with her best friend and husband, Dale, and when not quilting, she enjoys spending time with her children and grandchildren.

2. Sew the light and medium diamonds together beginning and ending stitches 1/4" from edge. (**Diagram 17**)

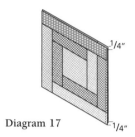

Diagram 17

3. Place dark and medium diamonds right sides together. Beginning 1/4" from the outside edge, sew toward inside corner, stopping 1/4" from end. (**Diagram 18**)

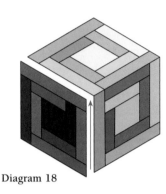

Diagram 18

4. Repeat step 3 sewing the dark diamond to the light diamond. (**Diagram 19**)

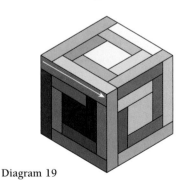

Diagram 19

5. Repeat steps 1 to 4 for remaining nine Diamond Log Cabins.

6. Sew blocks together in rows, again beginning and ending 1/4" from ends. (**Diagram 20**)

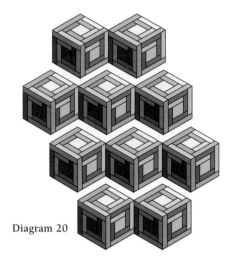

Diagram 20

7. Sew rows together. Remember to always begin and end sewing 1/4" from edges.

8. Cut a piece of fabric that is larger than the quilt top. (**Diagram 21**)

Diagram 21

9. Cut the fabric piece in half and sew it back together leaving a 15" opening in center. (**Diagram 22**) Press seam open.

10. Place pieced backing right sides together with quilt top. With quilt top facing up, sew around entire edge. Trim backing even with quilt top edges, clipping inside seams. (**Diagram 23**) Do not turn right side out at this time.

11. Cut a piece of batting to fit just inside the seam line; place on top of quilt top. (**Diagram 24**)

Diagram 22

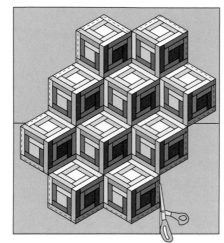

Diagram 23

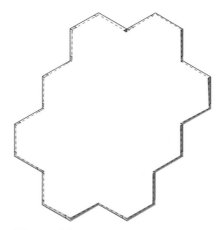

Diagram 24

Note: *Do not sew the batting down.*

12. Turn the quilt right side out through the opening. Smooth out edges of batting. Stitch the opening closed being careful not to catch quilt top in your stitching.

13. Quilt the layers together by hand or machine.

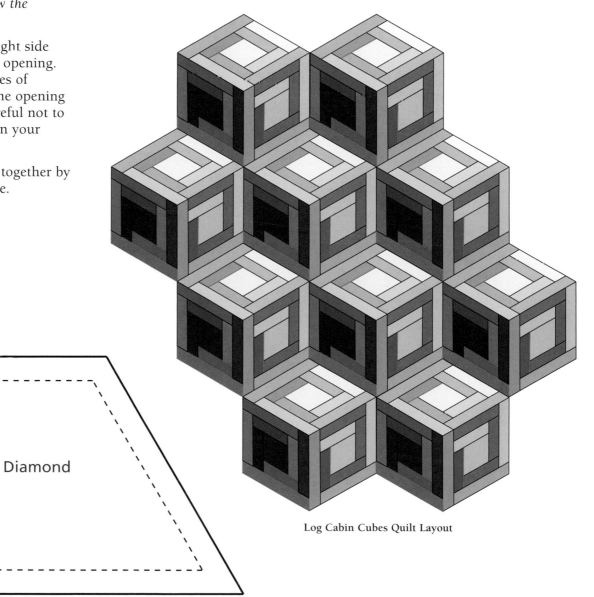

Log Cabin Cubes Quilt Layout

Diamond

107

Sometimes—as with this quilt—it's the fabric that determines the pattern. One look at the celestial prints from Northcott Silks, and the designer knew this was the perfect choice for a star Log Cabin. Each star is framed with dark green strips, and the entire quilt is framed with a wonderful celestial border print.

Celestial Star Log Cabin

by Linda Causee

Approximate Size
50^1/2" x 50^1/2"

Materials
^{1}/3 yard turquoise
1^1/4 yards purple
^{1}/2 yard dark green (includes first border)
^{3}/8 yard dark orange
^{5}/8 yard light green
^{3}/4 yard light orange
1^1/2 yards border print (second border)
^{1}/2 yard binding
3 yards backing
batting

Pattern
Log Cabin ^{1}/4 Star Foundation Pattern, page 110

Cutting
Note: *You do not have to cut exact pieces when foundation piecing. Cut strips in the widths shown below for easier piecing.*

Blocks
4 strips, 2^1/2"-wide, turquoise (center 1)
9 strips, 2"-wide, purple (spaces 2, 3)
9 strips, 1^1/8"-wide, dark green (space 4)
9 strips, 2^3/8"-wide, purple (space 5)
4 strips, 1"-wide, light green (space 6)
4 strips, 1^1/2"-wide, light green (space 7)
4 strips, 1^1/4"-wide, dark orange (space 8)
5 strips, 2^1/4"-wide, dark orange (space 9)
6 strips, 1^1/2"-wide, light orange (space 10)
7 strips, 1^3/4"-wide, light orange (space 11)

A quilt editor for a needlework publishing company since 1990, **Linda Causee** designed her first quilt book in 1996. Since then she has authored over 30 quilt books using various quilting techniques.

Although foundation piecing, the technique used here, is her personal favorite technique, Linda has written books on many other quilting techniques including appliqué, crazy quilts, redwork, and postage stamp quilting.

A graduate of the University of California, Linda makes her home in Oceanside, California in a house filled with quilts.

Finishing
4 strips, 1¹/4"-wide, dark green (first border)
4 vertical strips, 7"-wide, border print
     (second border)
5 strips, 2¹/2"-wide, binding

Instructions

1. Make 36 Log Cabin foundations referring to
    Preparing the Foundation, page 154. (**Diagram 1**)

2. Referring to Making a Foundation Block, pages
    152 to 154, piece the blocks referring to the
    pattern for placement of colors. (**Diagram 2**)

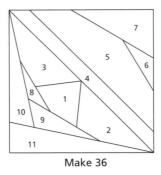

Make 36

Diagram 1

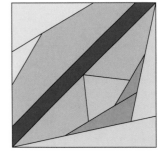

Diagram 2

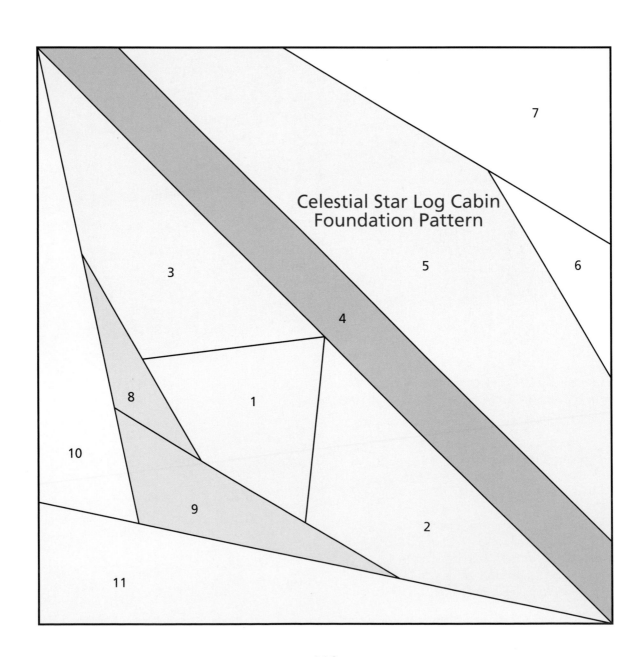

Celestial Star Log Cabin
Foundation Pattern

3. Sew blocks together in pairs then sew pairs together to form Star blocks. (**Diagram 3**)

4. Place blocks in three rows of three blocks. Sew together in rows then sew rows together.

5. Measure quilt lengthwise; cut 1¹/₄"-wide dark green strips to that length. Sew to sides of quilt. Measure quilt crosswise; cut 1¹/₄"-wide dark green strips to that length. Sew to top and bottom of quilt.

6. Refer to Mitered Borders, page 154, to add 7"-wide border print strips.

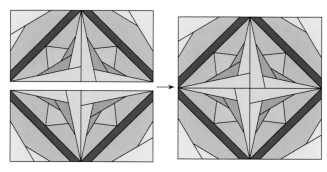

Diagram 3

7. Refer to Finishing Your Quilt, pages 154 to 159, to complete your quilt.

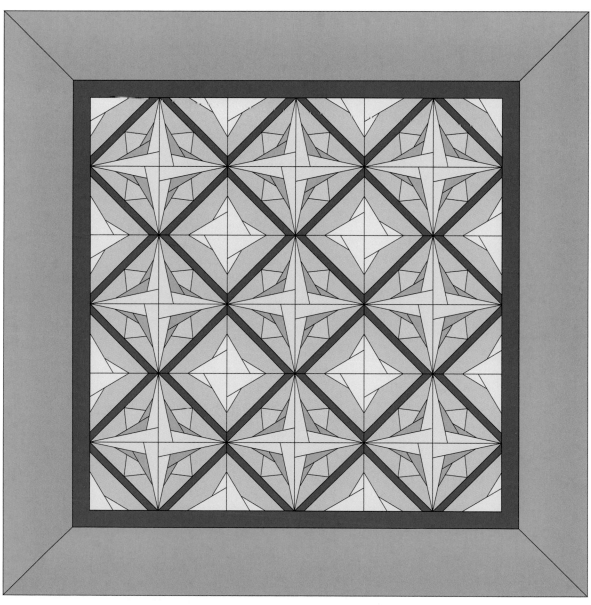

Celestial Star Log Cabin Quilt Layout

This Log Cabin was designed as an answer to the friend who demanded an immediate introduction to quilting so that she could make a present for a baby shower; a quilt that would require no measuring, no perfect points and could be made from scraps because she had no money. Here is the perfect block! It can be made from scraps, requires no measuring, little planning and can be completed quickly. One block becomes a pillow; several blocks become a quilt.

World's Easiest Log Cabin

by Stacy Michell

Materials (for a pillow)
1/2 yard muslin or light colored fabric
assorted hand-dyed scraps and fat quarters
1/2 yard backing
12" pillow form

Cutting (for one block)
12 1/2" square, muslin
2 rectangles, 7 1/2" x 12 1/2"

Instructions

Note: *Make one block for a pillow or several blocks for a wall hanging.*

1. Fold and press an "X" in to the muslin foundation. (**Diagram 1**)

Diagram 1

2. Cut assorted fabric into wedges. Cut wedges into assorted sizes. (**Diagram 2**)

Note: *Don't cut straight strips. Everything is slightly askew.*

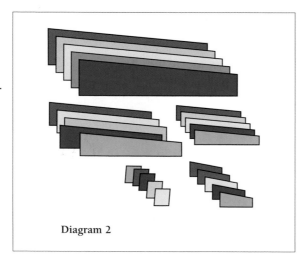

Diagram 2

After visiting several large quilt shows **Stacy Michell** was inspired to explore the options of hand-dyed textiles in the quilting marketplace. In 1986, she began her business venture, "Shades Textiles."

Stacy was uniquely qualified for the job of textile artist. As a child she began sewing at age four, received her first sewing machine when she was six and made her first quilt at ten. In addition, she was an avid finger painting artist and loved the touch and feel of paint and the swirls of color, as they mixed with each other on paper—very much like the fabric she produces today.

Stacy began exhibiting at quilt shows, and at the Houston Quilt Market, she met a Japanese textile artist, who encouraged her to enter the export market place. Today much of her fabric is sold in Japan, and can be found in many prize-winning quilts.

Currently Stacy lives and works in Marietta, Georgia where Shades Textiles occupies a 3600 square foot studio.

Stacy's friend, for whom she designed this block, completed over six of these quilts—one of them a California King—leaving Stacy's sewing room a disaster and her scrap bags depleted. Today her friend is allowed to visit the studio, but she must sew at home. As Stacy says, "Some friends are friends because they have a huge heart and an incredible recipe for Key Lime pie!"

A traditional Log Cabin quilt in a new guise! Just large enough to be a cover for a special doll, this tiny quilt is slightly less than a 15" square. Each block is only 2" square, but it is easily pieced using the foundation piecing method. Placement of color in the outer blocks gives the appearance of an inner dark blue border without actually piecing a border.

Log Cabin Mini
by Linda Causee

Approximate Size
$14^1/2$" x $14^1/2$"

Materials
$1/8$ yard dark pink
$3/8$ yard light multi-color swirl
$1/4$ yard medium blue
$1/2$ yard dark blue (includes border and binding)
fat quarter backing
batting

Patterns
Log Cabin A, page 119
Log Cabin B, page 119

Cutting
Blocks
Note: *You do not have to cut exact pieces when foundation piecing. Cut strips in the widths shown below for easier piecing.*

16 squares, 1" x 1", dark pink (Log Cabin A centers)
1 strip, $7/8$"-wide, dark pink (Log Cabin A corner blocks)
4 squares, 1" x 1", light multi-color swirl (Log Cabin A)
8 strips, $7/8$"-wide, light multi-color swirl (Log Cabin A and Log Cabin B)
16 squares, 1" x 1", medium blue (Log Cabin B centers)
4 strips, $7/8$"-wide, medium blue (Log Cabin A and Log Cabin B)
3 strips, $7/8$"-wide, dark blue (Log Cabin A and Log Cabin B)

Finishing
2 strips, $1^1/2$" x $12^1/2$", dark blue (border)
2 strips, $1^1/2$" x $14^1/2$", dark blue (border)
2 strips, $2^1/2$"-wide, dark blue (binding)

When Linda Causee was attending the University of California, she helped to pay for her tuition by working as an accountant. It might have been that attention to detail that is reflected in her appreciation of foundation piecing miniature quilts.

Foundation piecing is one of Linda's favorites, and as she says, "The only way I'd piece something this small."

When she's not quilting or writing quilt books, Linda is probably wandering through fabric stores making fabric choices. "Any color works," she insists, "as long as it's blue."

Instructions

1. Make 20 Log Cabin A and 16 Log Cabin B foundations referring to Preparing the Foundation, page 151. (**Diagram 1**)

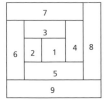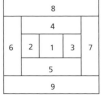

Make 20 Log Cabin A · · · Make 16 Log Cabin B

Diagram 1

2. For the center of the quilt, make four Log Cabin A1, four Log Cabin A2 and eight Log Cabin A3. (**Diagram 2**)

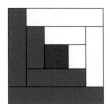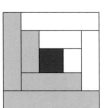

Block A1 - Make 4 · Block A2 - Make 4 · Block A3 - Make 8

Diagram 2

3. For border and corners, make four Log Cabin A4 and 16 Log Cabin B. (**Diagram 3**)

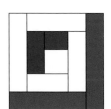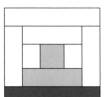

Block A4 - Make 4 · Block B - Make 16

Diagram 3

4. Place the center blocks in four rows of four blocks. Sew together in rows then sew rows together. (**Diagram 4**)

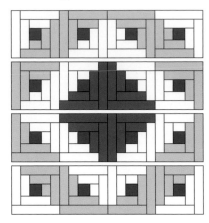

Diagram 4

5. Sew four border Log Cabin B blocks together; repeat three more times. (**Diagram 5**)

Diagram 5

6. Sew border strips to opposite sides of quilt. (**Diagram 6**)

Diagram 6

7. Sew a corner Log Cabin block A to opposite sides of remaining Log Cabin B borders; sew to top and bottom of quilt. (**Diagram 7**)

8. Sew $1^{1}/2$" x $12^{1}/2$" dark blue border strips to sides of quilt; sew $1^{1}/2$" x $14^{1}/2$" dark blue strips to top and bottom. (**Diagram 8**)

118

Diagram 7

Diagram 8

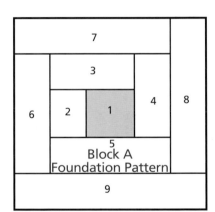

Block A
Foundation Pattern

7

3

6 2 1 4 8

5

9

Log Cabin Mini Quilt Layout

9. Refer to Finishing Your Quilt, pages 154 to 159,
to complete your quilt.

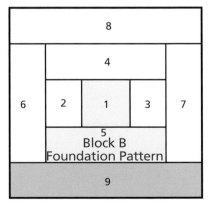

Block B
Foundation Pattern

8

4

6 2 1 3 7

5

9

This purple and turquoise quilt is made using the Pineapple pattern. Both the colors and the pattern are favorites of the designer. While set differently than the traditional Log Cabin quilt, the Pineapple is definitely a Log Cabin version with its "logs" set at an angle. One of many Log Cabins created by this designer, this quilt was made as a gift to the designer's brother and sister-in-law.

Purple Pineapple

by Dori Hawks

Approximate Size
76" x 76"

Materials
$2^1/2$ yards turquoise/purple print (includes fourth border)
2 yards light turquoise solid
2 yards assorted purple
$3/4$ yard turquoise print (includes second border)
$1^1/4$ yards purple print (first border and binding)
$4^1/2$ yards backing
batting

Patterns
Log Cabin Pineapple Foundation (Left half), page 124
Log Cabin Pineapple Foundation (Right half), page 125

Cutting
Blocks
25 squares, 2" x 2", turquoise/purple print (space 1)
9 strips, 2"-wide, turquoise/purple print (spaces 42-45)
50 strips, $1^1/4$"-wide, light turquoise solid (spaces 2-5, 10-13, 18-21, 26-29, 34-37)
13 strips, $1^1/4$"-wide, turquoise print (spaces 38-41)
35 strips, $1^1/4$"-wide, assorted purple (spaces 6-9, 14-17, 22-25, 30-33)

Finishing
5 strips, $3^1/4$"-wide, purple print (first border)
6 strips, $1^1/4$"-wide, turquoise print (second border)
45 strips, $1^1/4$"-wide, assorted purple (third border)
8 strips, $7^1/2$"-wide, turquoise/purple print (fourth border)
9 strips, $2^1/2$"-wide, purple print (binding)

Taught to sew at an early age, **Dori Hawks** even took a sewing machine to college where she majored in Health and Physical Education. After college Dori worked as the Art Director for the Easter Seal Society of Houston, but she was always sewing—making all of her clothes, shirts for her sons, and even business suits for her husband. Eventually she began teaching sewing at shops in the Houston area.

Quilting came into her life in the mid 1980's after attending her first Quilt Festival in Houston. Despite the fact that she was alone and knew no one, her enthusiasm knew no bounds. She went back on Friday, Saturday and finally brought her husband on Sunday. She looked at him earnestly and said, "I know you are not going to understand this, but I found what I want to do for the rest of my life!"

For over 20 years, Dori has been involved with quilting and teaching. Over two years ago she began an online quilting magazine, www.theQuilterCommunity.com. She writes, designs patterns and edits material for posting on her website. In addition, she has written two quilt books, *A Quilters Book of Baskets* and *Signed by Friends.*

Instructions

Blocks

1. Trace both halves of pattern and tape together. Pattern should measure 9" x 9". Make 25 foundations. (**Diagram 1**)

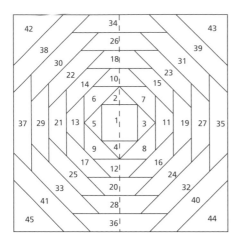

Diagram 1

2. Piece 25 blocks using cut strips. (**Diagram 2**)

Diagram 2

Finishing

1. Place blocks in five rows of five blocks. (**Diagram 3**)

Diagram 3

2. Sew blocks together in rows. Press seams for rows in alternating directions. Sew rows together.

3. For first border, measure quilt lengthwise. Piece and cut $3^1/4$"-wide purple print strips to that length. Sew to sides of quilt. Measure quilt crosswise. Piece and cut $3^1/4$"-wide purple print strips to that length. Sew to top and bottom of quilt.

4. Repeat step 3 for second border using $1^1/4$"-wide turquoise print strips.

5. For third border, sew five $1^1/4$"-wide assorted purple strips together to form a strip set. (**Diagram 4**) Repeat with remaining purple strips.

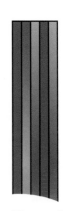

Diagram 4

6. Cut strip sets at $5^1/2$" intervals. (**Diagram 5**)

7. Measure quilt lengthwise. Sew $5^1/2$" purple segments together until correct length is achieved. Repeat for another strip. Sew to sides of quilt.

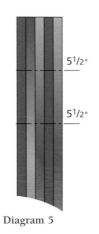

$5^1/2$"

$5^1/2$"

Diagram 5

8. Measure quilt crosswise. Sew $5^1/2$" purple segments together until correct length is achieved. Repeat for another strip. Sew to top and bottom of quilt.

9. Repeat step 3 for fourth border using $7^1/2$"-wide turquoise/purple print strips.

10. Refer to Finishing Your Quilt, pages 154 to 159, to complete your quilt.

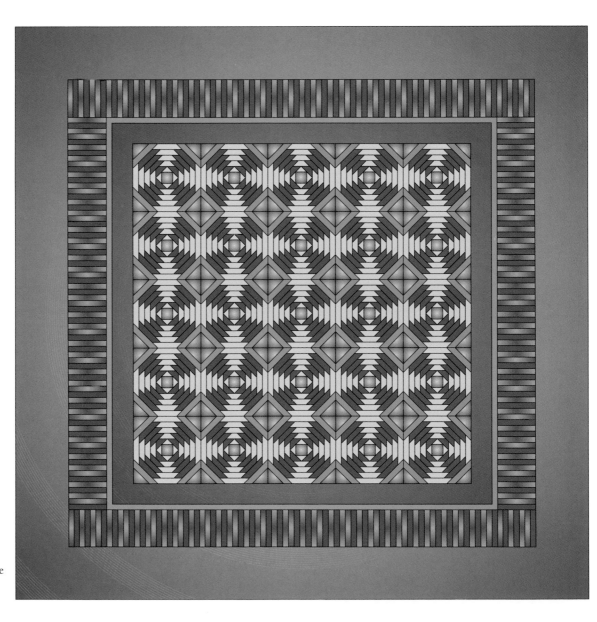

Purple Pineapple
Quilt Layout

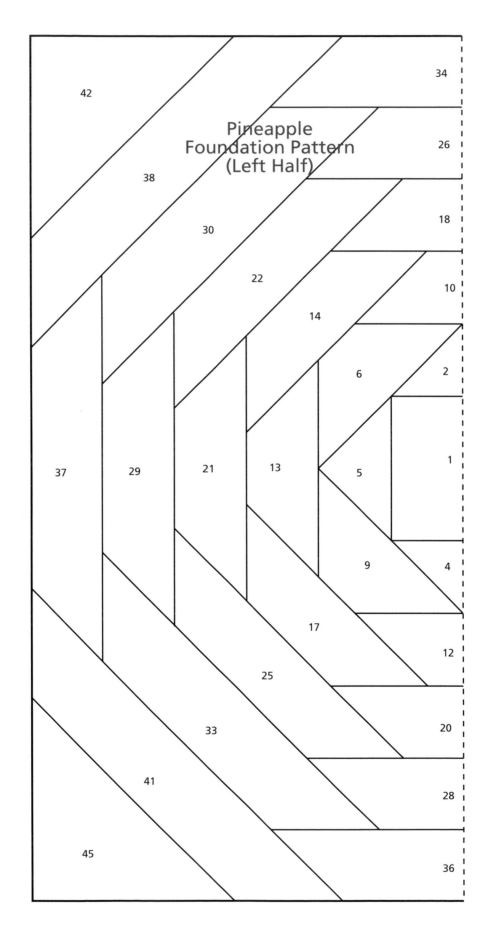

Pineapple
Foundation Pattern
(Left Half)

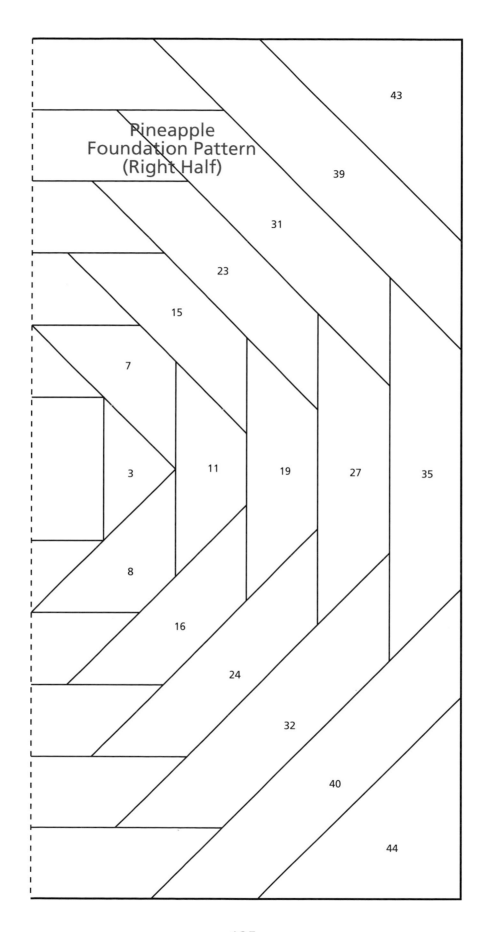

Pineapple
Foundation Pattern
(Right Half)

125

Made of flannel fabric depicting Alaskan wildlife and co-ordinating flannel prints, this quilt pays homage to our 50th state. Different Log Cabin blocks were designed to fit around the centers of various sizes. Two layers of flannel were used for each "log". The rag effect was achieved by sewing with the wrong sides together allowing the seams to be on the right side. The seams were then clipped and fluffed in the dryer.

Alaska Rag
by Linda Causee

Approximate Size
72" x 72"

Materials
$1^1/2$ yards novelty flannel print (You may need more or less yardage depending on the spacing of the individual motifs on your fabric.)
$1/2$ yard yellow flannel
$3/4$ yard beige flannel
1 yard dark blue flannel
1 yard blue floral flannel
$7/8$ yard blue leaf print flannel
$7/8$ yard brown paw print flannel
1 yard green flannel
$5/8$ yard red print flannel
8 yards backing flannel (Use the same fabric for the entire backing or for more interest, buy fabrics that correspond to the fabrics and amounts of those used on the front.)

Cutting
Block 1 (Mountains)
6 strips, $3^3/4$" x 5", mountain motif (center)
12 strips, $2^1/2$" x 5", blue leaf print (logs 1, 2)
12 strips, $2^3/4$" x $6^3/4$", dark blue (logs 3, 4)
12 strips, $2^1/2$" x $8^1/2$", blue floral (logs 5, 6)
12 strips, $3^7/8$" x $9^3/4$", dark blue (logs 7, 8)
12 strips, $2^5/8$" x 13", blue leaf print (logs 9, 10)

Block 2 (Squirrel)
4 squares, 4" x 4", squirrel motif (center)
4 strips, $3^1/4$" x 4", blue leaf print (log 1)
4 strips, $3^1/4$" x $6^1/4$", blue leaf print (log 2)
4 strips, $3^1/4$" x $6^1/4$", green (log 3)
4 strips, $3^1/4$" x $8^1/2$", green (log 4)

On a recent trip to Alaska, while the rest of the family was seeing the sights, **Linda Causee** could be found visiting fabric stores, wherever she could find them. In Ketchikan she not only discovered a quilt shop, but an idea was born for a wonderful quilt that would become a souvenir of the trip. In that shop she found the fabrics used to make this quilt.

A fabric picturing Alaskan wildlife provides the centers for the quilt while co-ordinating flannel prints add the perfect finishing touch. Since the fabric was flannel, turning it into a "rag quilt" was a natural.

What better way to remember Alaska than to snuggle under this warm quilt!

The designer wished to create a Log Cabin block that would be unique when completed. She began by constructing a traditional block, but then cut each block in half diagonally. By sewing the blocks back together, she has created a novel way to make a Log Cabin in which the finished blocks can be rotated to create a completely different pattern.

Split Logs
by Ann Harnden

Approximate Size
35" x 43"

Materials
$1^1/4$ yards blue dots
$^7/8$ yard yellow dots
$^1/4$ yard lime green
$^1/4$ yard green/blue floral (first border)
$^5/8$ yard medium blue (second border and binding)
$1^1/4$ yards backing
batting

Cutting
Blocks
30 squares, 2" x 2", lime green
20 strips, 2"-wide, blue dots
15 strips, 2"-wide, yellow dots

Finishing
5 strips, $1^1/2$"-wide, green/blue floral (first border)
5 strips, $2^1/2$"-wide, medium blue (second border)
5 strips, $2^1/2$"-wide, medium blue (binding)

Ann Harnden has always loved needlework of all kinds. While working for a needlework publisher editing cross-stitch books, her love affair with quilting began. The publisher was preparing to publish a book by Marti Michell and thought it would be a good idea if Marti taught the staff her methods.

For Ann it was "love at first sight." She came out of that first class completely enraptured with quilting, and hasn't stopped since. For the past 15 years, quilting has become a way of life for Ann.

She is happy doing all of the steps involved in quilting from choosing the pattern and fabrics to cutting and sewing, quilting and finally adding the binding and the quilt label. Ann has always been a member of her local quilt guilds where she readily assists her fellow quilters with any of their quilting problems.

Instructions

Note: *Refer to Strip Piecing Log Cabin Blocks, pages 149 to 150, before beginning.*

Blocks

1. Sew 2"-wide yellow dots strip (log 1) and 2"-wide lime green strip (c) together. Press seam to one side. Cut at 2" intervals. Sew pair of squares to 2"-wide yellow dots strip for log 2. Continue sewing strips in order around center referring to **Diagram 1**.

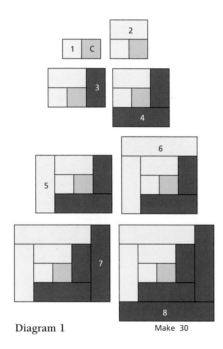

Diagram 1   Make 30

2. Cut a diagonal line on finished block. (**Diagram 2**) Repeat for all 30 blocks.

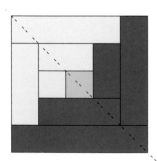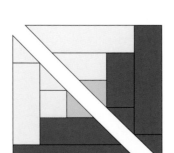

Diagram 2

3. Place resulting triangles in two stacks. (**Diagram 3**)

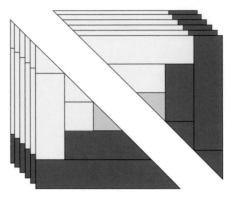

Diagram 3

4. Starting with one stack, sew together two triangles. (**Diagram 4**) You will have 15 Block A.

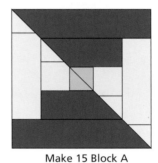

Make 15 Block A

Diagram 4

5. Sew together triangles from remaining stack until you have 15 Block B. (**Diagram 5**)

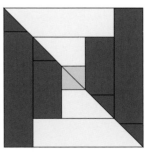

Make 15 Block B

Diagram 5

134

Finishing

1. Place blocks in six rows of five blocks. Sew blocks together in rows then sew rows together.

2. Measure quilt lengthwise. Cut two 1$\frac{1}{2}$"-wide green/blue floral strips to that length. Sew to sides of quilt. Measure quilt crosswise. Cut two 1$\frac{1}{2}$"-wide green/blue floral strips to that length. Sew to top and bottom of quilt.

3. Repeat step 2 for second border using 2$\frac{1}{2}$"-wide medium blue strips.

4. Refer to Finishing Your Quilt, pages 154 to 159, to complete your quilt.

Split Logs Quilt Layout

135

This whimsical quilt is made up of Log Cabin blocks with logs that are slightly askew. Colorful floral prints are foundation-pieced onto a paper foundation, then sewn together to make a wonderful garden maze.

Log Cabin Crazy Garden

by Linda Causee

Approximate Size
$38^1/2$" x $38^1/2$"

Materials
$3/4$ yard multi-color floral (includes binding)
$1/2$ yard yellow floral
1 yard green floral (includes second border)
$5/8$ yard purple floral
$1/2$ yard turquoise floral
$3/4$ yard blue floral
$3/8$ yard red floral (first border)
$1^1/4$ yards backing
batting

Patterns
Large Log Cabin, page 142
Small Log Cabin, page 143

Cutting
Note: *You do not have to cut exact pieces for foundation piecing. However, it is easier to piece if you cut strips, then piece and cut as you sew.*

Large Log Cabin blocks
1 strip, $2^1/2$"-wide, multi-color floral (centers)
5 strips, $1^3/4$"-wide, yellow floral (spaces 2, 3, 4 and 5)
4 strips, $1^5/8$"-wide, green floral (logs 6, 7)
3 strips, $1^7/8$"-wide, purple floral (log 8)
4 strips, $2^1/2$"-wide, purple floral (log 9)
6 strips, $1^1/2$"-wide, turquoise floral (logs 10, 11)
7 strips, $2^5/8$"-wide, blue floral (logs 12, 13)

While **Linda Causee** is best known for her foundation piecing, she is also a lover of crazy quilts and the author of several books on the subject including *Learn to Make a Crazy Quilt, An Encyclopedia of Crazy Quilt Stitches and Motifs,* and *101 Crazy Quilt Blocks.*

In this quilt she has combined her love of foundation piecing and her fascination with crazy quilts by creating these blocks that follow the Log Cabin rules but are created in a crazy style.

Traditionally a crazy quilt was never intended to provide warmth but rather to show the skills of the maker. They usually appeared as throws in the parlor rather than as covers for the beds.

While Linda likes to think of this as a Log Cabin Crazy Garden because of the floral fabrics used, a small dog prefers to think of it as the perfect spot from which to watch the world.

Small Log Cabins

1 strip, $1^1/2$"-wide, multi-color floral (centers)
4 strips, $1^1/4$"-wide, yellow floral (spaces 2, 3, 4 and 5)
2 strips, $1^1/8$"-wide, green floral (logs 6, 7)
1 strip, $1^1/8$"-wide, purple floral (log 8)
1 strip, $1^1/2$"-wide, purple floral (log 9)
3 strips, $1^1/4$"-wide, turquoise floral (logs 10, 11)
3 strips, $1^5/8$"-wide, blue floral (logs 12, 13)

Finishing

2 strips, 2" x $28^1/2$", red floral (first border)
2 strips, 2" x $31^1/2$", red floral (first border)
4 strips, 4" x $27^1/2$", green floral (second border)
5 strips, $2^1/2$"-wide, binding

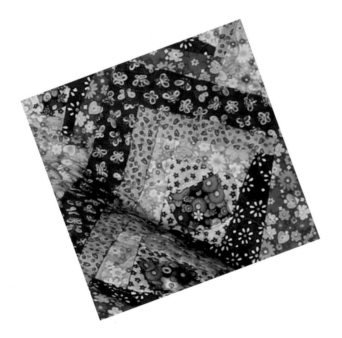

Instructions

1. Make 16 Large Log Cabin foundations and 12 Small Log Cabin foundations using patterns on pages 142 and 143. (**Diagram 1**)

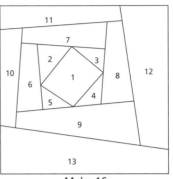

Make 16

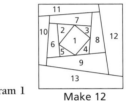

Diagram 1

Make 12

2. Make all Large Log Cabin blocks and Small Log Cabin blocks. (**Diagram 2**)

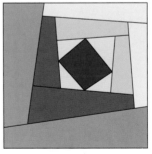

Make 16

Diagram 2

Make 12

Diagram 3

Diagram 4

Diagram 5

3. Place Large Log Cabin blocks in four rows of four blocks. Sew together in rows then sew rows together. (**Diagram 3**)

4. Sew 2" x 28^1/$_2$" red floral strips to opposite sides of quilt; press seams toward border. Sew 2" x 31^1/$_2$" red floral strips to top and bottom of quilt; press seams toward border. (**Diagram 4**)

5. Sew a Small Log Cabin block to opposite ends of each 4" x 27^1/$_2$" green floral strip. (**Diagram 5**)

6. Sew two border strips to opposite sides of quilt. (**Diagram 6**)

Diagram 6

7. Sew a Small Log Cabin block to each end of remaining border strips. Sew to top and bottom of quilt. (**Diagram 7**)

8. Refer to Finishing Your Quilt, pages 154 to 159, to complete your quilt.

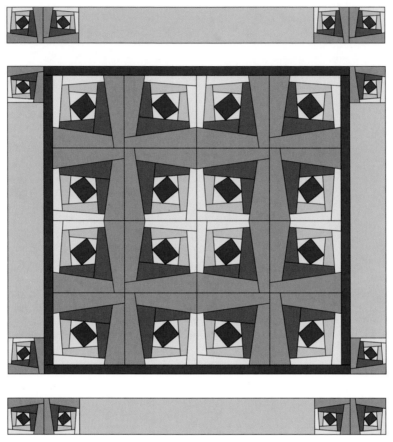

Diagram 7

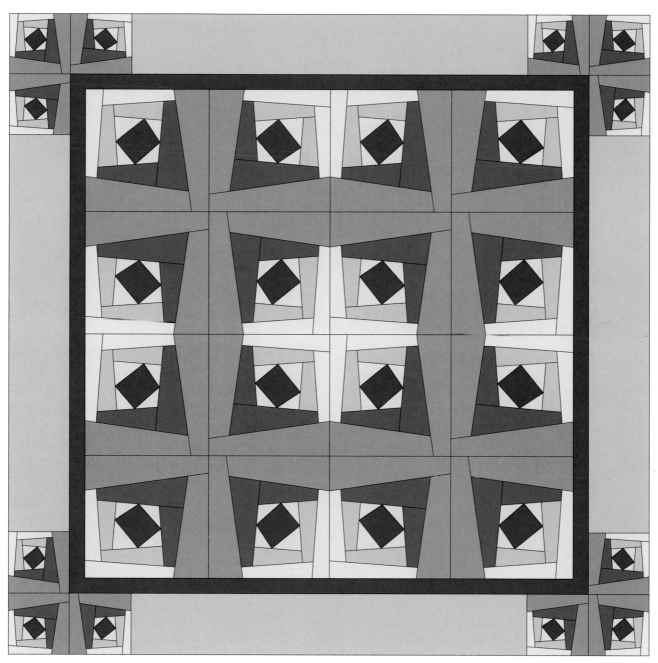

Log Cabin Crazy Garden Quilt Layout

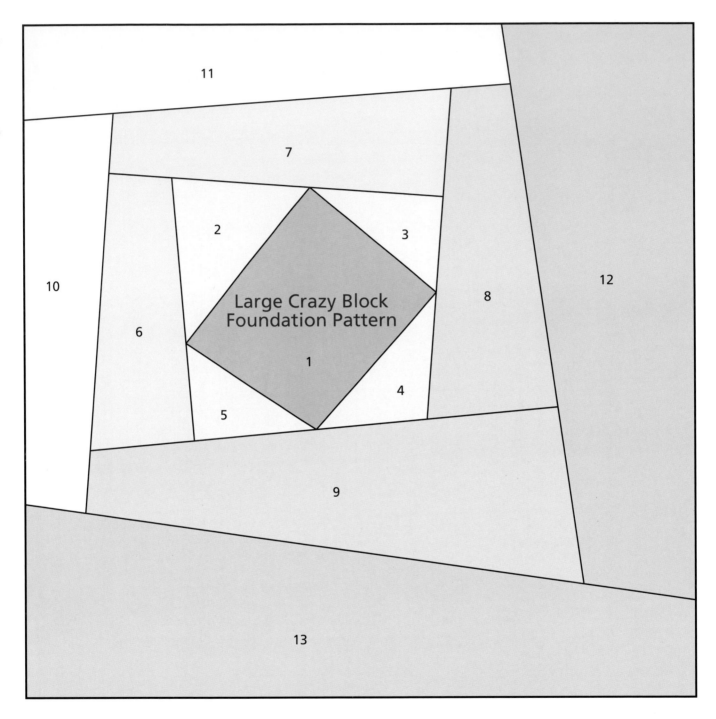

Large Crazy Block
Foundation Pattern

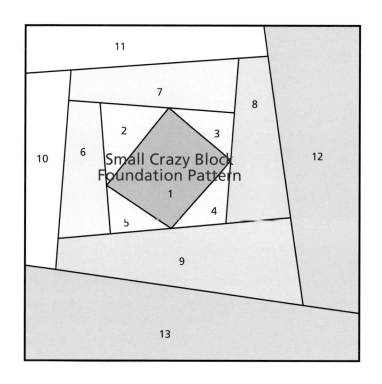

Small Crazy Block
Foundation Pattern

General Directions

Fabric

Old time quilts were traditionally made of 100% cotton and this is still the fabric that today's quilters prefer. Cotton has a number of properties that makes it suitable for patchwork. You will find less distortion with cotton fabric which means that your carefully cut pieces will fit together more easily. If you make a mistake and find a puckered area, a quilt made from 100% cotton often can be ironed flat with a steam iron. In addition, the sewing needle moves through cotton with ease as opposed to some synthetics. If you are hand quilting, this is an extremely valuable quality.

Pre-washing fabric is not necessary, but it is important to test your fabric to make certain that the fabric is colorfast and preshrunk (don't trust those manufacturer's labels). Start by cutting a 2"-wide strip (cut crosswise) of each of the fabrics that you have selected for your quilt. Measure the strips. To determine whether the fabric is color-fast, put each strip separately into a clean bowl of extremely hot water, or hold the fabric strip under hot running water. If your fabric bleeds a great deal, all is not necessarily lost. It might only be necessary to wash all of the fabric until all of the excess dye has washed out. Fabrics which continue to bleed after they have been washed several times should be eliminated.

Fabric should also be tested for shrinkage. Take each saturated strip from the colorfastness test above and iron it dry. Measure the strips and compare the measurements to the original measurement. The fabric industry allows about 2% shrinkage in cotton fabrics. That means that your fabric strips should not lose more than 1". If all of the strips shrink the same amount, then you really have no problem. If one of your fabrics is shrinking more than the others, it should be discarded.

Cutting the Fabric

Log Cabin blocks are made up of strips that surround a center square. Although the strips and squares can be cut with scissors, using a rotary cutter, mat and acrylic ruler will eliminate the use of templates, will cut the time spent cutting and piecing in half and most importantly, will make cutting and piecing more accurate.

1. Before cutting strips with a rotary cutter, your fabric must first be straightened. Fold fabric in half with selvages even—the cut edges may not be even at this time; fold fabric in half again with folded end even with selvages.

2. Carefully place your folded fabric on the cutting mat, lining up the folded edge along one of the horizontal lines of your mat. If you are right handed, the bulk of the fabric should be to the right of the edge you are straightening; if you are left handed, it should be to the left. (**Diagram 1**)

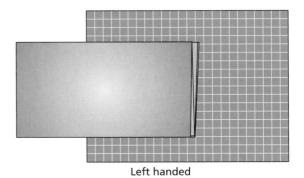

Left handed

Right handed

Diagram 1

3. Place your ruler on the fabric, lining up one of the crosswise markings of the ruler along the folded edge of the fabric; the long edge of the ruler should line up next to the cut edge. Press down firmly on the ruler and cut off the uneven edge. (**Diagram 2**)

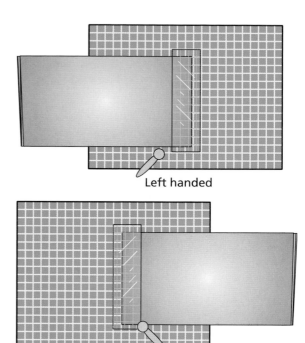

Left handed

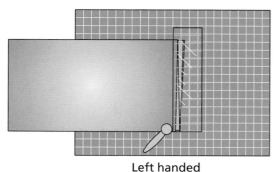

Left handed

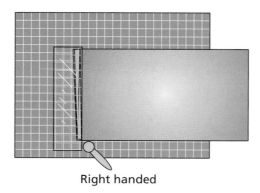

Right handed

Diagram 2

Right handed

Diagram 3

4. Now that you have made the initial cut, use this edge to align additional measurements. Place your ruler along the edge just straightened, lining up the correct measurement line on your ruler (the finished width of the "logs" plus 1/2" for seam allowance) with the straight edge of the fabric; cut your strip. (**Diagram 3**) **Note:** *Be sure that your ruler is always aligned with the folded edge as well as the cut edge of fabric.*

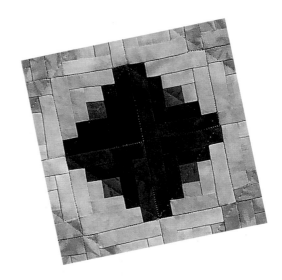

Making a Log Cabin Block

1. If making a traditional Log Cabin block with three rounds of 2"-wide finished "logs," you will need to cut the following squares and strips for each block:

    1 square, $2^1/2$" x $2^1/2$", center fabric (center)

    1 square, $2^1/2$" x $2^1/2$", light fabric (log 1)

    2 strips, $2^1/2$" x $4^1/2$", one each of light and dark (logs 2, 3)

    2 strips, $2^1/2$" x $6^1/2$", one each of light and dark (logs 4, 5)

    2 strips, $2^1/2$" x $8^1/2$", one each of light and dark (logs 6, 7)

    2 strips, $2^1/2$" x $10^1/2$", one each of light and dark (logs 8, 9)

    2 strips, $2^1/2$" x $12^1/2$", one each of light and dark (logs 10, 11)

    1 strip, $2^1/2$" x $14^1/2$", dark (log 12)

2. Place center square and light square 1 right sides together; sew along one edge. (**Diagram 4**) Press seam toward log 1. (**Diagram 5**)

Diagram 4   Diagram 5

3. Turn unit just made so that square (log) 1 is on the bottom and place right sides together with the light log 2; sew. Press seam toward log 2. (**Diagram 6**)

Diagram 6

4. Turn unit again so that log 2 is on the bottom and place right sides together with dark log 3; sew. Press seam toward log 3. (**Diagram 7**)

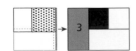

Diagram 7

5. Turn unit so that log 3 is on the bottom and place rights sides together with dark log 4; sew. Press seam toward Log 4. (**Diagram 8**)

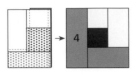

Diagram 8

6. Continue turning unit counterclockwise and sewing strips in numerical order. (**Diagrams 9** to **16**) Always press seams toward last strip (log) sewn.

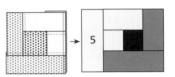

Diagram 9

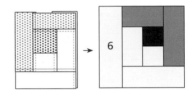

Diagram 10

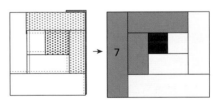

Diagram 11

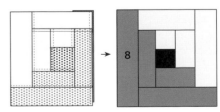

Diagram 12

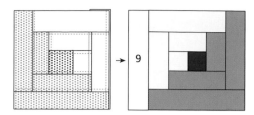

Diagram 13

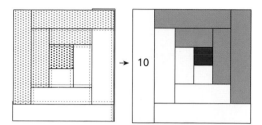

Diagram 14

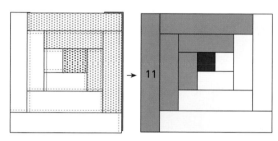

Diagram 15

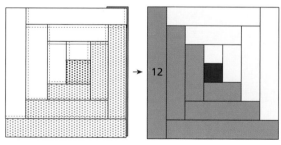

Diagram 16

7. Carefully press completed block and square up if necessary. To square up block, place your acrylic ruler so that markings are parallel to the longest seam. (**Diagram 17**) Trim edge if uneven.

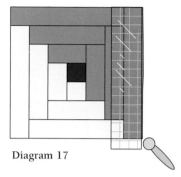

Diagram 17

8. Place short edge of ruler even with just-trimmed edge. **Note:** *The length of the ruler should be parallel to the lengthwise seams of the block. Trim edge if uneven.* (**Diagram 18**) Continue in same manner along remaining two sides.

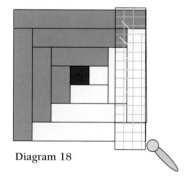

Diagram 18

9. Make remaining blocks for your project.

Chain Piecing

1. Cut strips according to step 1 above.

2. Place a center square and Log 1 right sides together; sew along one edge. (**Diagram 19**) Do not remove from sewing machine and do not lift presser foot.

Diagram 19

3. Place another center square and Log 1 right sides together; butt up against squares just sewn and continue sewing. (**Diagram 20**) Continue feeding pairs of squares under the presser foot until all center squares are sewn to Log 1.

Diagram 20

4. Clip threads between sewn pairs and press seam toward Log 1.

5. Place a pair of squares (Log 1 at the bottom) right sides together with a light Log 2; sew. (**Diagram 21**) Do not remove from sewing machine and do not lift presser foot.

Diagram 21

6. Place another pair of squares right sides together with light Log 2; butt up against unit just sewn and continue sewing. (**Diagram 22**) Repeat for remaining pairs of squares and Log 2.

Diagram 22

7. Clip threads between sewn units and press seam toward Log 2.

8. Add remaining strips in same manner until all blocks are finished.

9. Square up blocks referring to steps 7 and 8 page 147.

Strip Piecing Log Cabin Blocks

1. Cut all fabrics into the width specified in your instructions. For this example, cut $2\frac{1}{2}$"-wide strips. Cut along the crosswise grain of the fabric.

2. Place a center fabric strip right sides together with a light Log 1 strip; sew along one long edge. (**Diagram 23**) Press seam toward Log 1.

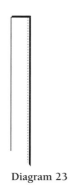

Diagram 23

3. Cut across strip set at $2\frac{1}{2}$"-wide intervals. (**Diagram 24**)

Diagram 24

4. Repeat steps 2 and 3 until you have the number of pairs of squares needed for the number of blocks you are making.

5. Place Log 2 strip right side up; put a pair of squares right side down on strip so the Log 1 is at bottom; sew. (**Diagram 25**) Do not remove from sewing machine and do not lift presser foot.

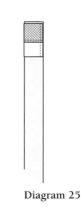

Diagram 25

6. Place another pair of squares on Log 2 strip below the pair just sewn and sew. (**Diagram 26**)

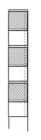

Diagram 26

7. Continue adding pairs of squares along Log 2 strips.

8. Press open. **Hint:** *Place units just sewn on ironing surface with strip side up. Press along seam, then press strip open.* (**Diagram 27**)

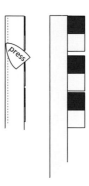

Diagram 27

9. Cut units apart using edge of squares as a guide for a straight cut. (**Diagram 28**)

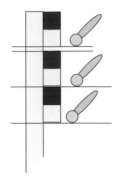

Diagram 28

10. Place unit just sewn right sides together with Log 3 strip so the Log 2 is at the bottom; sew. (**Diagram 29**)

Diagram 29

11. Place another unit on Log 3 and continue sewing. (**Diagram 30**)

Diagram 30

12. Continue adding units along Log 3 strips. Press, then cut units apart.

13. Add remaining strips in same manner until block is complete. (**Diagram 31**) Square up block referring to steps 7 and 8 on page 147.

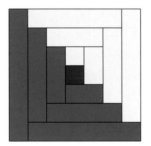

Diagram 31

Foundation Piecing a Log Cabin Block

Foundation Material

Before you begin, decide the kind of foundation on which you are planning to piece the blocks. The most popular choice is paper. It's readily available and fairly inexpensive. You can use copy paper, newsprint, tracing paper—even computer paper. The paper does not remain a permanent part of your quilt as it is removed once the blocks are completely sewn.

You can also use fabric as your foundation, especially if you choose to hand piece your block. Just remember that fabric is not removed after you make your block so you will have another layer to quilt through. This may be a problem if you are planning to hand quilt. Using fabric might be an advantage, however, if you want to use some non-traditional quilting fabrics, such as satin, since the fabric foundation will add stability to the block. If you do decide to use fabric, choose a lightweight and light-colored fabric, such as muslin, that will allow you to see through for ease in tracing.

Another option for foundation materials is Tear Away or Fun-dation™, translucent non-woven materials combining the advantages of both paper and fabric. They are easy to see through but like paper they can be removed with ease.

Currently a new kind of foundation material has appeared in the market place: a foundation paper that dissolves in water after use. Two companies, W.H. Collins and EZ Quilting by Wrights are producing this product.

Preparing the Foundation

Place your foundation material over the block pattern and trace. Use a ruler and a fine-line pencil or permanent marker, and make sure that all lines are straight. Sometimes short dashed lines or even dotted lines are easier to make. Be sure to copy all numbers. You will need to make a foundation for each block you are planning to use.

If you have a home copier, you can copy your block from the book right onto the paper that can then be used for the foundation. Since the copy machine might slightly alter the measurements of

the block, make certain that you copy each block from the original pattern.

You can also scan the block if you have a home scanner and then print out the required number of blocks.

Cutting the Fabric

In foundation piecing, you do not have to cut perfect shapes.

You can, therefore, use odd pieces of fabric: squares, strips, rectangles. The one thing you must remember, however, is that every piece must be at least $1/4$" larger on all sides than the space it is going to cover. Strips and squares are easy: just measure the length and width of the needed space and add $1/2$" all around. Cut your strip to that measurement. Triangles, however, can be a bit tricky. In that case, measure the widest point of the triangle and cut your fabric about $1/2$" to 1" wider.

Other Supplies for Foundation Piecing

Piecing by hand:

You will need a reasonably thin needle such as a Sharp Size 10, a good quality neutral-colored thread such as size 50, some pins, a glue stick, fabric scissors, muslin or fabric for the bases.

Piecing by machine:

You will need a cleaned and oiled sewing machine, glue stick, pins, paper scissors, fabric scissors, foundation material.

Hint: *Before beginning to sew your actual block by machine, determine the proper stitch length. Use a piece of the paper you are planning to use for the foundation and draw a straight line on it. Set your machine so that it sews with a fairly short stitch (about 20 stitches per inch). Sew along the line. If you can tear the paper apart with ease, you are sewing with the right length. You don't want to sew with such a short stitch that the paper falls apart by itself. If you are going to use a fabric foundation with the sewing machine, use the stitch length you normally use.*

151

Making the Foundation Block

The important thing to remember about making a foundation block is that the fabric pieces go on the unmarked side of the foundation while you sew on the printed side. The finished blocks are a mirror image of the original pattern.

1. Hold the foundation up to a light source—even a window pane—with the unmarked side facing. Find the space marked 1 on the unmarked side and put a dab of glue there. Place the fabric right side up on the unmarked side on Space 1, making certain that the fabric overlaps at least 1/4" on all sides of space 1. (**Diagram 32**)

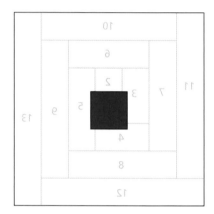

Diagram 32

2. Fold the foundation along the line between Space 1 and Space 2. Cut the fabric so that it is 1/4" from the fold. (**Diagram 33**)

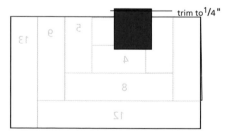

Diagram 33

3. With right sides together, place Fabric Piece 2 on Fabric Piece 1, making sure that the edge of Piece 2 is even with the just-trimmed edge of Piece 1. (**Diagram 34**)

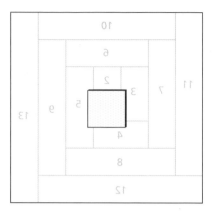

Diagram 34

4. To make certain that Piece 2 will cover Space 2, fold the fabric piece back along the line between Space 1 and Space 2. (**Diagram 35**)

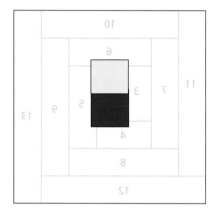

Diagram 35

5. With the marked side of the foundation facing up, place the piece on the sewing machine (or sew by hand), holding both Piece 1 and Piece 2 in place. Sew along the line between Space 1 and Space 2. (**Diagram 36**)

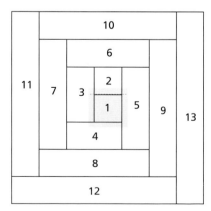

Diagram 36

Hint: *If you use a small stitch, it will be easier to remove the paper later. Start stitching about 2" to 3" before the beginning of the line and end your sewing 2" or 3" beyond the line, allowing the stitches to be held in place by the next round of stitching rather than by backstitching.*

6. Turn the work over and open Piece 2. Finger press the seam open. (**Diagram 37**)

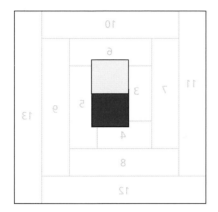

Diagram 37

7. Turning the work so that the marked side is on top, fold the foundation forward along the line between Space 1+2 and Space 3. Trim about 1/8" to 1/4" from the fold.

Hint: *It is easier to trim the paper if you pull the paper away from the stitching. If you use fabric as your foundation, fold the fabric forward as far as it will go and then start to trim.*

8. Place Piece 3 right side down even with the just-trimmed edge. (**Diagram 38**)

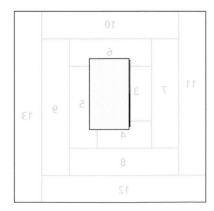

Diagram 38

9. Turn the block over to the marked side and sew along the line between Space 1+2 and Space 3. (**Diagram 39**)

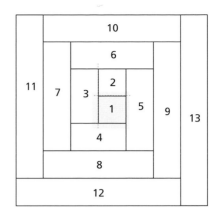

Diagram 39

10. Turn the work over, open Piece 3 and finger press the seam. (**Diagram 40**)

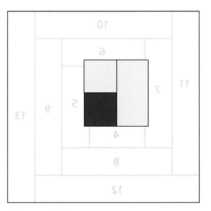

Diagram 40

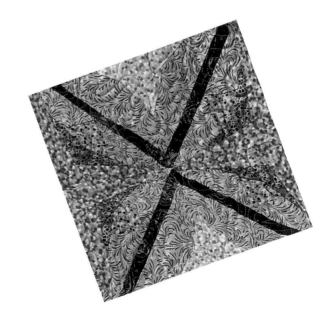

11. Add remaining pieces in same manner to complete this block. Trim the fabric 1/4" from the edge of the foundation. The foundation-pieced block is completed. (**Diagram 41**)

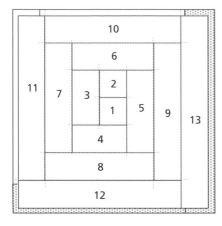

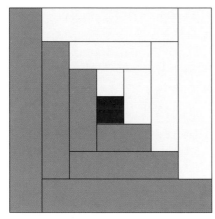

Diagram 41

After you have finished sewing a block, don't immediately remove the paper. Since you are often piecing with tiny bits of fabric, grainline is never a factor. Therefore, some of the pieces may have been cut on the bias and may have a tendency to stretch. You can eliminate any problem with distortion by keeping the paper in place until all of the blocks have been sewn together. If, however, you want to remove the paper, stay stitch along the outer edge of the block to help keep the block in shape.

Finishing Your Quilt

Adding Borders

Piecing Border Strips

To achieve necessary length of border strips, you may have to piece strips together. The best way to do this to make the resulting seam less noticeable, is to piece the strips diagonally. Place two strips right sides together at a right angle. Sew from corner to corner diagonally. Trim about 1/4" from sewing line and press seam open. (**Diagram 42**)

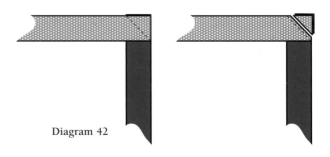

Diagram 42

Simple Borders

1. Measure quilt lengthwise. Cut two border strips to that length. Sew to the sides of the quilt top.

2. Measure quilt crosswise. Cut two borders to that length. Sew to the top and bottom of the quilt top.

3. Repeat steps 1 and 2 for additional borders.

Mitered Borders

1. Measure the quilt top lengthwise. Sew together two border strips diagonally then cut two strips that length plus twice the finished border width plus 1/2" for seam allowances. For example, if the quilt length measures 50 1/2" and the finished border width is 4", you will need to cut the border strips 50 1/2" + 4" + 4" + 1/2" or 59".

2. Measure the quilt top crosswise. Piece and cut two strips that length plus twice the finished border width plus 1/2".

3. Find the midpoint
   of a border strip
   by folding strip
   in half.
   (**Diagram 43**)

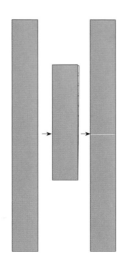

Diagram 43

4. Place strip right
   sides together with
   quilt top matching
   midpoint of border
   with midpoint of
   quilt side. Pin in
   place.
   (**Diagram 44**)

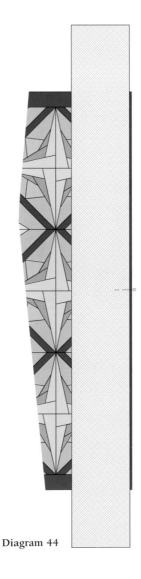

Diagram 44

5. Place pin ¹/4" from top and bottom edges of
   quilt top, then pin entire border to quilt.

6. Beginning at first pin, sew border strip to quilt
   top ending at last pin. Backstitch at beginning
   and ending of sewing. (**Diagram 45**)

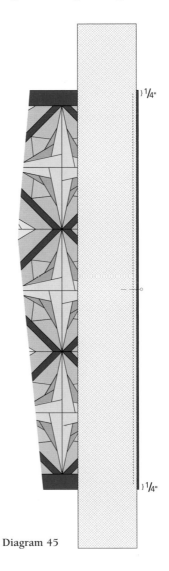

Diagram 45

7. Repeat steps 3 to 6 at remaining three sides.

8. To finish corners, fold quilt top in half diagonally; borders will extend straight up and away from the quilt. Place a ruler along folded edge of quilt top going into border strip; draw a diagonal line on border. (**Diagram 46**)

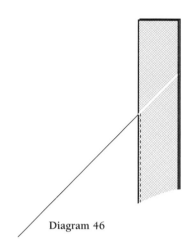

Diagram 46

9. Beginning at corner of quilt top, stitch along drawn line to edge of border strip. (**Diagram 47**)

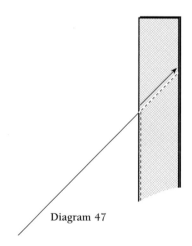

Diagram 47

10. Open quilt at corner to check miter. If satisfied, trim excess fabric $1/4$" from diagonal seam. (**Diagram 48**) Repeat steps 8 and 9 at remaining three corners.

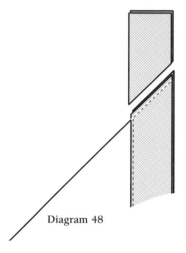

Diagram 48

Attaching the Batting and Backing

There are a number of different types of batting on the market today including the new fusible battings that eliminate the need for basting. Your choice of batting will depend upon how you are planning to use your quilt. If the quilt is to serve as a wall hanging, you will probably want to use a thin cotton batting. A quilt made with a thin cotton or cotton/polyester blend works best for machine quilting. Very thick polyester batting should be used only for tied quilts.

The best fabric for quilt backing is 100% cotton fabric. If your quilt is larger than the available fabric, you will have to piece your backing fabric. When joining the fabric, try not to have a seam going down the center. Instead cut off the selvages and make a center strip that is about 36" wide and have narrower strips at the sides. Seam the pieces together and carefully iron the seams open. (This is one of the few times in making a quilt that a seam should be pressed open.) Several fabric manufacturers are now selling fabric in 90" or 108"-widths for use as backing fabric.

It is a good idea to remove the batting from its wrapping 24 hours before you plan to use it and open it out to full size. You will find that the batting will now lie flat when you are ready to use it.

The batting and the backing should be cut about one to two inches larger on all sides than the quilt top. Place the backing wrong side up on a flat surface. Smooth out the batting on top of this, matching the outer edges. Center the quilt top, right side up, on top of the batting.

Now the quilt layers must be held together before quilting, and there are several methods for doing this:

Safety-pin Basting: Starting from the center and working toward the edges, pin through all layers at one time with large safety pins. The pins should be placed no more than 4" apart. As you work, think of your quilting plan to make sure that the pins will avoid prospective quilting lines.

Thread Basting: Baste the three layers together with long stitches. Start in the center and sew toward the edges in a number of diagonal lines.

Quilt-gun Basting: This handy trigger tool pushes nylon tags through all layers of the quilt. Start in the center and work toward the outside edges. The tags should be placed about 4" apart. You can sew right over the tags, which can then be easily removed by cutting them off with scissors.

Spray or Heat-Set Basting: Several manufacturers have spray adhesives available especially for quilters. Apply these products by following the manufacturers' directions. You might want to test these products before you use them to make sure that they meet your requirements.

Fusible Iron-on Batting: These battings are a wonderful new way to hold quilt layers together without using any of the other time-consuming methods of basting. Again, you will want to test these battings to be certain that you are happy with the results. Follow the manufacturers' directions.

Quilting

If you like the process of hand quilting, you can—of course—finish these projects by hand quilting. However, if you want to finish these quilts quickly, you may want to use a sewing machine for quilting.

If you have never used a sewing machine for quilting, you may want to find a book and read about the technique. You do not need a special machine for quilting. Just make sure that your machine has been oiled and is in good working condition.

If you are going to do machine quilting, you should invest in an even-feed foot. This foot is designed to feed the top and bottom layers of a quilt evenly through the machine. The foot prevents puckers from forming as you machine quilt. Use a fine transparent nylon thread in the top and regular sewing thread in the bobbin.

Quilting in the ditch is one of the easiest ways to machine quilt. This is a term used to describe stitching along the seam line between two pieces of fabric. Using your fingers, pull the blocks or pieces apart slightly and machine stitch right between the two pieces. The stitching will look better if you keep the stitching to the side of the seam that does not have the extra bulk of the seam allowance under it. The quilting will be hidden in the seam.

Free-form machine quilting can be used to quilt around a design or to quilt a motif. The quilting is done with a darning foot and the feed dogs down on the sewing machine. It takes practice to master free-form quilting because you are controlling the movement of the quilt under the needle rather than the sewing machine moving the quilt. You can quilt in any direction—up and down, side-to-side and even in circles—without pivoting the quilt around the needle. Practice this quilting method before trying it on your quilt.

Attaching the Continuous Machine Binding

Once the quilt has been quilted, the edges must be bound. Start by trimming the backing and batting even with the quilt top. Measure the quilt top and cut enough $2^{1}/2$"-wide strips to go around all four sides of the quilt plus 12". Join the strips end to end with diagonal seams and trim the corners. Press the seams open. Cut one end of the strip at a 45-degree angle and press under $^{1}/4$". (**Diagram 49**)

On the back of the quilt, position the binding in the middle of one side, keeping the raw edges together. Sew the binding to the quilt with the $^{1}/4$" seam allowance, beginning about three inches below the folded end of the binding. (**Diagram 51**)

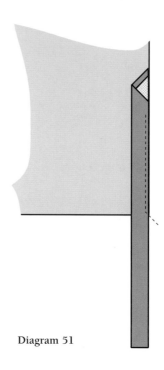

Diagram 51

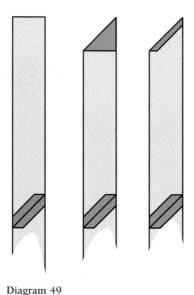

Diagram 49

Press entire strip in half lengthwise, wrong sides together. (**Diagram 50**)

At the corner, stop $^{1}/4$" from the edge of the quilt and backstitch.

Fold binding away from quilt so it is at a right angle to edge just sewn. (**Diagram 52**)

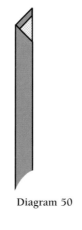

Diagram 50

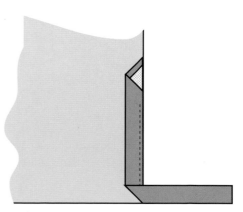

Diagram 52

Then, fold the binding back on itself so the fold is on the quilt edge and the raw edges are aligned with the adjacent side of the quilt. Begin sewing at the quilt edge. (**Diagram 53**)

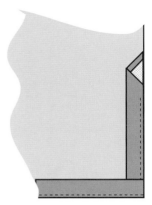

Diagram 53

Continue in the same way around the remaining sides of the quilt. Stop about 2" away from the starting point. Trim any excess binding and tuck it inside the folded end. Finish the stitching. (**Diagram 54**)

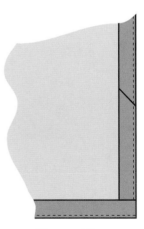

Diagram 54

Fold the binding to the front of the quilt so the seam line is covered; machine-stitch the binding in place on the front of the quilt. Use a straight stitch or tiny zigzag with invisible or matching thread. If you have a sewing machine that does embroidery stitches, you may want to use your favorite stitch.

Always sign and date your quilt when finished. You can make a label by cross-stitching or embroidering or even writing on a label or on the back of your quilt with a permanent marking pen. If you are friends with your computer, you can even create an attractive label on the computer.